OFFERINGS:

A SPIRITUAL POETRY ANTHOLOGY

FROM TIFERET JOURNAL

D1287137

Course taught by Donna Baier Stein

Poems written by participants in
Tiferet's Writing Workshops 2020-2022

DEDICATION

This anthology is dedicated to Mary-Lynne Monroe

Alpha and Omega
-in honor of Mary-Lynne Monroe

Where we have to go is somewhere hard to see.
It calls our name, sings to us
long before the day
our shiny head pierces
the veil of the womb ...
our slippery, sloshy, sing-songy orb —
or is it heart shaped?

Snuggling the not-yet-baby
only a few cells
Do they know what they will become?

Then the boomerang shape of the spine
Does it know what it will become?

Then the wandering fingers
nubs that press outward, onward
Do they know what they will craft?

Soon they will reach for yours
those groping fingers without purpose yet,
already reaching
always reaching ...

Soon we will reach for them
delighting in the soft curl of newly shaped hands
as they learn from their grasp of what is solid.

We learn endlessly about what is solid,
our eyes resting on the hook of the moon
so far from touch, but we know it is there,
as dense as our own planet, denser than touch,
made from stardust and the cosmic exhale.

Does the moon know what it is becoming?

Does it
matter?

Where we have to go from the very beginning
is a constant steady beautiful march toward the end
that never comes, the end that circles back unto itself,
the snake hungering its own tail.

And if we go willingly, nothing solid can stop us.

-Cit Ananda

INTRODUCTION

By Donna Baier Stein

We held our first Spiritual Poetry gathering in March 2020. The reality of the pandemic was taking hold, and I imagined that offering an online zoom class might be one way to be of service. I wanted to provide community in the face of isolation. And I wanted to share poems that had special meaning to me, that had helped me through hard times.

I had no idea that the class I designed as a gift to others would prove to be a gift to myself as well.

Because Tiferet is an interfaith publication, I had access to poems from every tradition and because of the wonders of the internet, access to spiritual poets from every era.

As I said to the first poets who gathered that early spring, you didn't have to believe in God to be there. You might find the sacred taking a walk in the woods. You might find it in a church, a synagogue, a mosque, a desert in Israel, a shrine at home, a retreat center, a painting, a symphony, your heart.

For me, spirituality is about viewing this material world from a higher perspective. This higher perspective may be embodied in an entity like God or Yahweh or Allah or Krishna, or it might be named consciousness or energy or the universe or Brahman.

We started by gathering once a week for one and a half hours. I prepared Powerpoint slides with three poems and after reading each poem, gave the attendees, the poets, ten minutes of silence to freewrite to a prompt I provided.

What happened during those ten minutes I think astonished all of us.

There were a few poets who had published, and many who had not. But because of the poems and because of the atmosphere of the group and because of the people themselves, each one was truly able to make of themselves a conduit, like Rumi's flute.

Each poet had a chance to read two of the three poems they had written to the group. Sometimes tears were shed; sometimes laughter. And we kept going. Facing our fears about the virus or the state of the world or the physical and mental health of ourselves and our loved ones. Everything and everyone was welcome. And the poems transcended the daily news that weighed us down.

We've now met – in various configurations of people – for more than 2.5 years. We've heard poets from India, New Zealand, Wales, Israel, British Columbia, and across the United States. There are stalwarts who sign up for each six-week session, for whom I am grateful.

Because this gathering in sacred space to write is a co-creation. Somehow during that hour and a half together we sometimes manage to transcend into what I sometimes call The Upper Room, even while holding the challenges of the human world.

My hope is that these poems written during short ten minute stretches speak to you. My hope is that you see the common threads among religions and recognize the many paths to spirit, to transcendence, to love.

Special thanks to our Managing Editor Lisa Sawyer, designer Donna Schmitt, and Anthology Committee members who made this project come to life:
Cit Ananda Fowler, Molly Howes, Tom Hedt, Joanell Serra, Gabriela Iñiguez, Bambi Koeniger, Betty Johnson, and Amy Small-McKinney.

FROM OUR WEBSITE:
Tiferet is a Hebrew word that, in my opinion, describes a state from which true creativity arises. I think of it as being similar to the

razor's edge envisioned by Somerset Maugham—a balancing of heaven and earth, good and evil, opposing forces that don't usually reconcile. On the kabbalistic Tree of Life, tiferet is a stable center where the physical and spiritual realms meet.

My decision to publish a magazine called TIFERET came about as one of the ordinary miracles that make up our lives.
It can be no accident that the Word holds such significance in many world religions and spiritual practices. "In the beginning was the Word" proclaims John 1:1 in the New Testament. According to kabbalah, or Jewish mysticism, letters themselves have special powers; there is divine mystery behind the drawing and placement of each letter. Those who practice Siddha Yoga worship the goddess Matrika, the sacred power behind every sound and every letter. And, as Nobel Peace Prize winner, Shirin Ebadi, points out, the first sermon in Islam begins with the word, "Recite!"... and, she went on to say, "The Koran swears by the pen and what it writes. Such a sermon and message cannot be in conflict with awareness, knowledge, wisdom, freedom of opinion and expression and cultural pluralism."

The mission of our magazine, then, is to help reveal Spirit, in all its manifestations, through the Written Word. We publish writing from authors of many faiths, even non-traditional ones.

My hope is that TIFERET will indeed help foster cultural pluralism... help us all in our own search for and communion with divinity... and be a stable center within our modern lives, a place where the flames of creativity burn brightly.

May you find sustenance—spiritual, emotional, literary—in our community.

CONTENTS

Horizons

I contemplate spirals
seeking / not seeking
climbing /it's never a straight line
up the steep face
Hatcher Pass
at solstice.

Waiting
watching
evening take the day
a long slow dusk
its 10 PM, it won't get dark.
I sit on a rock
I savor
isolation
wonder.

When the sun returns,
change happens quickly here,
everything   loosened,
water flows this time of year
Fishhook Creek, the Little-Su, the Matanuska,
choked with sediment - glacial four,
it's all awake, come to life.

The horizon before me
is a sharp ridge
it is orange,
the sun moves along it
not down into it
as if time were oblique
opaque
diagonal
episodic
a caterpillar spinning

The World Awaits
from John O'Donohue

Sunflowers shadow
a patch of green, their faces
black plates ringed gold.

An iron bench beside
a statue of Mother Mary
invites me to pause, breathe in

a pair of Great Blues
as they sail through the sun;
their legs like matchsticks
ignite the lake.

The mind kindles
with scars inflicted, vows broken
but the world awaits
the day that is here.

At water's edge, I sound
a low D on a Lakota blessed flute,
gift from a neighbor who
this morning on her porch
whistled daybreak.

-Karen Luke Jackson

All Days Are Not Bright

the heart is heavy
with the burden of corruptible love
it tosses in sleep
moans and groans
against waking light.
the gray day
helps.
things in the garden
will be quenched
by rain
so as not to need
my care,
today.
there are times
when we must delay
our deepest longing
admit the lingering despair
that hangs around
like cloudy skies
we know will break
again, for the golden light.

all days are not bright
but by the heart's
necessary grieving
made lighter.

what can we notice
about the righteousness
of this seeming imperfection?
may we know purer love
through doubts' days of cloudiness

and the dampening rains of sadness
come to relieve our dry ground
waiting beneath the hiding sun
which will return
to warm all creatures
with its glowing clarity.

-Elizabeth Graham

Reaching for a life we do not know

There is a life we do not know of
Or
Most do not know of,
Shhhhhhhhh!
Let's not spread the word
Because I find such pleasure and sanity
In talking to lizards
Speaking to bats
Petting hedgehogs
And often
I so wish
I had more time in their lives
In their world
This human one
Often bleak
Theirs seems simpler
Sometimes easier
The Praying Mantis on our patio
Waits not for
The Muezzin
Or the Church bells
Or the Shabbat sunset siren
To beckon prayer
Always sacred
Always holy
As he moves with such elegance
From Jasmine
To Gooseberry
To Roses
Reaching
Always reaching those long green

Magically hinged
Arms and legs
Towards God
And
I too reach.
Shhhhhhhhhh.

-Tammy Einstein

When I Contemplate the Moon

I remember the Chinese who set parenthesis
to bracket each new season, the space set aside
as earth swings into a new home beneath the stars.

"Everything will feel upside down and
inside out at such a time," a friend tells me.

Yet the Equinox comes and goes and the sun
and moon find time in equal measures
to do their thing: to energize and relax,
to move ahead and fall behind.

"I've taken to moon bathing," my friend
tells me. "The yin energy will restore
a wounded tired soul."

I am skeptical until I walk outdoors
one night in the early stages of your illness
and find a grandmother moon waiting for me
peeking down beyond a bowl of autumn clouds.

She holds my head until all thoughts
disappear, she floods my heart until
my fears flee. A light rain begins to fall.

-Marijo Grogan

Useless

What is my work in the world?

This world, this very one
where hard things happen
and grief pools around us.

This world where the hawk sits at dawn on the treetop
Waiting, the morning hunt.

Where the yellow green buds of the ancient oak again appear,
regardless.

Grasshoppers, disturbed
by the weight of boots in the tall grass,
not yet mowed.

What is my work here in this world?

To hold open the space,
observe the turning of the earth.

To bear witness to it all,
the beauty that explodes,
Laughing at my effort to name it.

To be pulled back once again
by the rising sun
Beyond any human work, assumed roles.

To stand,
Useless in the face of God.

-Betty Johnson

When I Despair for Our Suffering World

I leave the square space
of the walls that surround me
and spend time with oaks and maples
I admire the polished sheen of chestnuts
in a ferment of yellow leaves
I drink in the warmth of weakening sunlight
like the last drops of a rare oolong

I sit with these my friends
still, in their rooted presence
I listen to their quiet voices
And I think...
If healing will come to the world
If transforming words will come
they will surely be spoken
in the language of trees

-Allison Douglas-Tourner

Far From the Frantic World I Am

I am a witness to the reawakening of the world's conscience.
Smoke softens my view today, though I am days from the wildfires.
Opinions discombobulate the nations, though my country is at peace.
An illness changes our path, even though I know no one who is sick.

A worshipper of nature, I hear trees rustling with the breath of change.
Steam bubbles out of the hill announcing new birth and innocence.
Mountains stand too vast to capture their royal girth with my camera.
A silence so holy and ancient I feel like falling to my knees.

I am witness, and worshipper, part of nature, in and of the world.
I am the ground, the air, and the path on which I am lost.
Birds serenading become a part of me, and I am a part of them. Far
from the frantic world I rest and am restored, absorbed.

-Leah C. Mueller

Still We Stand

The circular wooden tombstone,
carved with your ancient name
in concentric rings,
stands with phantom height,
calling attention to your former majesty, Tree—
your great girth, your stubborn solidity.

The shadow of your shadow
somehow cools me,
even without your branches or leaves
to block the afternoon sun
as I stand upon your stump,
my arms outstretched, tree-like.

Green energy shoots from your ancient roots
through my human feet
into my own still standing trunk,
and we merge, beyond species, beyond time periods,
into a natural relativity that sprouted long ago,
into a cycle foretold by
the rings on which I stand.

-Susan L. Lipson

Like An Orange

When new, it's tender,
juicy sweet to the lips.
Thick or thin, you only need a fingernail
to peel away its skin.

I had the chance to tell it, while we waded
through the surf
and breezes lifted confidences
to drift toward open ears.

We left the wave-washed shore
and walked into the woods.
Hush-hush hissed the grasses.
Quiet, breathed the wind above.

When old, it's bitter to the tongue,
desiccate, decayed within.
Kept long and past its prime, you need a knife
to split its hardened rind.

-Teresa H. Janssen

Taking God Out of the Sky

After Chelan Harkin, The Worst Thing

Whoever thought of putting God in the sky?
How was God ever in the sky
  the unstructured,
    unformed eternal azure?
A dome, you say?
  How could that be?
Breath:
  each and every one
Slowly: In and out
  reveals God in me,
    touching you,
  as I speak to you.
The holiest thing we do is touch each other.
Trees, flowers, shimmering stars, moon, All emit
  that most essential piece of life.
God on the earth
  with every step.
My hand touching the earth, grass
  emits this essence.
Is there anywhere
  where God is not?

-Bambi Koeniger

The Holiness of Simplicity

Am I of use when I tend my garden,
choosing which weeds to pull,
leaving behind the Wild Thistle
and Joe-Pye Weed

fragrantly luring swallowtail butterflies
and bumble bees
to drink their
sweet nectar

Am I of use when I walk along
the beach hearing waves
lapping the shore,
lapping my feet

I long to be forever
in the ebb and flow of life,
to live each day like the
waves upon the shore,

one day laden with seaweed
so thick it stops me from moving forward,
another the water so clear,
I see the sand beneath my feet

-Lucinda Gadow

When the Dust Settles

When the dust settles, there will be no apology.

The sky will open with bird & cloud.

We will run along the Rio Grande as if born anew.

The wings of the ancients will flutter.

Dawn will appear like gold coins rising.

Can you hear the vibration, soft to the ear?

The sound of a rose blooming, each petal opening, & opening.

Now the scent of hyacinth & a blush to the cheek.

What else is there for us to do but love our lives?

We are sentinels to our own satisfactions.

Stand with me, our spines gentled.

Breathe desert air into the lungs.

We are everything, & we are nothing.

Stand firm.

Place your staff into the ground.

-Alicia Elkort

What I Cannot See

What I cannot see is
what makes the eagle rise
wings open
to flee its perch and
search for another.
Is it food or movement or
just stretching?
Is it need or curiosity?
       Can you imagine the eagle–
       royal, ancient, wise
       laser focused, powerful
       as curious?
Is it me that brings her out of her nest,
away from the branch?
My conviction that she
is a symbol, a conduit
for my friend's dead son?
       She appears so often
       in our grief
       he must be there
       reassuring us.
What else calls her from the treetops to dip above?
I cannot know, just as I cannot imagine why he chose to leave us
or why the eagle chooses to soar.

-Marla Mulloy

At the Base of the Old Cedar

I want to leave behind the icy winter
my encrusted footprints becoming mud.

I will take the path behind the sign
pointing humans in the opposite direction.

I will cast my sight across the grey valley
as it rediscovers fertility.

I will curve with ferns as we entice the sun
to stream fingers through our curls again.

Then pause at the base
of the old cedar

my hand on her shredding bark
stripped inside of me,

her broken branches, my stubborn knots,
her yielding crevices, my outstretched limbs.

Our roots intertwined
in the softening slope.

-Suzanne Doerge

Feathers

I once sat upon the water
light as a feather,
of the gull overhead.

Lightness can be scary. It's as if
we instinctively grasp for weight,
the ballast of our burden bag,
afraid that if we lost too many
burdens we would simply float away.

I have seen people float away.
The body crying out against
it, growing ever more possessive
until the sigh of relief - and the final
breath - moments after release.

The gull still floats above me,
each feather immaculate,
while I drift weightless
in my simple canoe.

-Thomas Hedt

Reconciliation

I build a room of tea leaves & heart-shaped lychee
to catalogue the ghosts of the past.

I'm closer to finding my way home which is to say
I reconcile with voices of the dead.

I sit in chest-high grass,
quiet as a line of assembled ants,
as unapologetic as a recurring dream.

The one where death waves a stony hand at me
from the crimson-flowered meadow.

Meanwhile, the sun sleepwalks all day.
Peace has no chance in the rattle of the world.

When did we become an incessant rumble?

If grief is the blood of the gun
hope is a theatre curtain waiting to rise.

I mollycoddle my hungry ghosts
into milksop & bird-bone.

Who can we pray to
when the earth is a fire of hollyhocks?

Which is to say, what really matters
is that one small kindness

and listening to the cardinal
aflame in song, aflame in pitch.

-Louisa Muniz

Sweet Potato

An unremarkable errand
to buy some milk,
I slow, as usual, to catch my familiar glimpse
of the sparkly lights of the City
through the trees in the gap
between the houses,
but then I stop altogether,
drawn by a flash
of other-worldly light
appearing and disappearing,
a giant red orb,
the moon,
the autumn moon, harvest
moon, harvest colored,
like russet potatoes, sweet potatoes,
round, fleshy, brilliant
in its reflection
of the autumn sun
that set at a new
October angle, leaving enough
light to burnish my moon,
my end-of-day, my reason to stop.
I want to touch, to hold it,
to roll it in my hands and then,
with a puff of air, blow it back into the sky
to lighten the burdens
of someone else on an unremarkable errand.

-Helen Mazarakis

Remembering More

I step out through the French doors
into the dark.
Lights above, tiny and wan, remind me:
there's more.

More than my eyes can see,
more than my ears can hear,
much more than my mind can grasp.
All day I grasp at nothings;
all day, I forget.

In the dark, I remember
and begin to see
the more.
The archer, the bull, the scorpion above,
coming clear as I stand,
hands raised through the darkness.
Ancient stardust in bones and sinew,
outlined against the light of More.

-Melanie Lynn Griffin

Anthropocene: Emergency Exit

After he's inspected the last bullet
train and signed off on another monochromatic
      factory, the architect of the imminent goes
      to bed dreaming he's an otter
      holding his beloved's hand on the water.

He imagines them as he once saw
on television, a dwindling tribe programmed
      to clasp each other in sleep. No matter
      the currents, the morning will wake
      to the familiar flute of the other.

In this dream, I will choose for myself
the shiver-and-snatch of a squirrel. My
      imaginary paws will bury acorns, and forget
      the spot. In my amnesia, I will leave behind
      forests of *prana* and nut-studded trunks.

It's not that improbable this side
of the world; in another life you might have been
      a penguin, offering your mate just a pebble
      for a proposal, one pellet holding
      enough fire and future to mate for life.

Or you might have lived in the lilt
of the butterfly, tasting nectar with your feet,
      knowing sweetness in all you land upon.
      Or one of a choir of birds. Or half of a pair
      of gibbons, the more moderate of our ancestors.

Instead, here we are, bipedal, opposable thumbed,
too much mind, too little wing, needing more
        than pebble promises, forgetting to forget
        the buried acorn, scraping the sky, excavating
        embers from a tired, sagging soil, dreaming

of an emergency exit, a yesterday, a tomorrow
        shaped
                like an otter,
                        a penguin,
                                a butterfly.

-Pervin Saket

Second Hope

Hope is the bird's nest
my son brought. One autumn day.
Smoke clouds covering.
Hills burning. Flaming fingers
lapping at the trunks of trees.

He ran toward me that
afternoon when fear drifted
through the air. I stood under
a live oak tree, poised.
Students holding pencils.

I watched him sprint from
the top of the hill, slowing
to a walk before pausing,
carefully placing the nest
in my hands, then smiling and
running away.

The night we unpacked, the
bird's nest was gone.

Yesterday, In the
gloom of a cool April day,
my son threw open the door.
He walked toward me where
I sat, writing beside a
hearth fire, flaming.

Holding a cradle
of twigs and down in his small,
strong hands, knowing I would thrill
at the sight. I would laugh out
loud. I would open my hands.

Wooly down warmed my
palms, my chilled, lonesome
fingers like fire never could.
My son filled my heart with his
sprint and his smile. My son filled
my hands with his hope.

-Jane O'Shields

The Nail Set

Cast steel, patterned gripping edges
worn through decades;
a familiar firm home to fingers that grasp it.
Flat point is rounded and smooth,
sets a nail with perfection;
no sliding, no drifting to mar perfect surfaces.

I was a young carpenter when my father
handed me this nail set from
a vast collection; his basement shop
smelled of must, dust, pipe smoke and crankcase oil.
Dad had rows of nail sets, but this was his best,
made for fine work. He expected me to use it well.

A nail not quite flush,
gently tapped firm,
with a fingertip of putty;
finished,
set.

-Margo Jodyne Dills

A Pact

Love is water
taking the shape of this vessel,
edges porous, flowing through our lips,
heating it to vapor.

We entered into a pact, you and I,
each signing over our past
for this present—which we unwrap
until we are naked.
Then holding our gift in the air,
we let the wind take it.

-David Breitkopf

Between the Lines

Rain has been falling all day
So many dashes and splashes
it sounds like static
a radio frequency
just out of range

During WWII my mother
intercepted Japanese messages
for the code breakers
higher up

The messages were in Morse
and also a secret code
that made everything a mystery
a jumble
Di dah di dah

In the rattling of water pipes
or the rhythm of footsteps in the hall
even in her sleep she heard...
mysterious messages from
out there somewhere

But she knew
that jumble and cypher were both there
It was all there and
it all meant something important
She just didn't know what

Now the rain blows against the glass
and I think of her
gone to a place beyond words
running lines, broken lines
Di dah di daaaaaaaaa

I open my window
and listen

-Allison Douglas-Tourner

A Wedding Poem

I wish for you the freshness of surprise,
for stories you haven't heard from each other,
for stories you haven't told,
for unfamiliar light on the planes of your beloved's cheek.

I wish for discovery again and again
of what endears you to each other,
of ways of being
that haven't yet become who you are.

I wish for moments like those first drops of rain
that spot your shoes and mess your glasses,
for soft mismatched pajamas
and unsuppressed hilarity at how ridiculous you look.

Maybe most of all
I wish you a tender bridge,
an edifice built of regret and repair,
of toothpicks and Elmer's glue,
a fragile thing but yours alone,
a bridge across the chasm
of "But I thought you meant – "
and "You just don't get it."
I wish for one (or the other) of you
to make a move,
a tiny tentative but necessary touch of the hand,
barely a breeze,
a silent flare,
a signal to say:
"I'm still with you.
I am still yours –
no! I am yours *again*.

I will reach for you again and again
and forever again."

I see the two of you
setting out on foreign and familiar paths,
side by side, hand in hand,
giving birth to your own heaven,
created again, anew.

-Molly Howes

For My Children

I give you my blessing.
Savor my words, repeat them,
with or without attribution,
if you need them.
Sprinkle them like sugar over dry yeast,
add warm water, and wait
until your own words
are spilling over the rim of the bowl.
Knead and press them into dough.
Form loaves to sustain you.

-Pamela Gottfried

Faith Is

Faith is sitting
on the edge of your mother's bed —
her white hair fragile as tissue paper —
holding her forehead while she heaves,
praying.

Faith is taking her temperature,
believing the thermometer works.
It's bringing her ginger ale and decongestant
and later Tylenol and toast,
making some rice to ease her stomach,
hoping it will heal.

Faith is seeing her watch some TV,
proof she's starting to feel better.
Then letting her go back to bed,
trusting she'll wake again.

One day you will lose this mother,
the best person to happen to you.
One day you will have to let her go,
the way too many already have.

Faith is believing that this Spring
outside our windows, and on our walks,
this Spring we cannot touch —
is real.

-Maria Giura

My Prayer for You

That angel-armies surround your path

That the sun warms you and guides your goings

That when you stumble, miracle stones encourage you

That when storms and fires come, you will not be crushed

That He's engraved your name on the gate of His memory

That He comforts you all the hours of the day, all days of the week,

 all months of the year — That His peace be honeyed: that He swathes

you in layers of grace and mercy and loving kindness

-Deborah Gerrish

The World That Awaits

You long for it, know it waits
think it's up to you
Call a car, convince a daughter
get dressed, pack your suitcase
wait in your wheelchair
one of the kids is coming
and you can relax
on your way west
past the wheat fields
buttes and badlands
going. going.
at each new city
a year drops off
going to Missoula
to the fir trees and the mountains
the goose who stole your bread
the cow who didn't like you
the feel of your bare toes
squishing warm cow patties
on cool mornings
your dad reading adventures
to you and your brothers
after supper
your mother churning butter
cooking on a wood stove
you're on your way
all you need is the driver
going to where someone will meet you
someone with open arms will greet you
someone's waiting there
to welcome you back home

-*Margaret Coombs*

54

To Be Human

is to fear abandonment, to
face the pain of being broken.

To be human is to be vulnerable.
Once you open your heart to another
human, you risk losing.

We are windswept,
braving rainstorms, floods, even tornadoes.
Everything can be lost.

To be human is to require sustenance,
not just food, but the nourishment
of holding hands.

We are expectant, hopeful.
We float downstream, arms open wide
We look for the slivers of sunlight
shining through the grasses.

-Christine Higgins

The Other World. This World.

To see the other world in this world was never a struggle.
You easily skipped in and out of both worlds.
Speaking with the angels, debating with the prophets.
Laughing and joking with the guides. Daily.

To see the other world in this world was never a question.
But as years passed, your star flickered and waned.
Your stride slowed. The world haunted you.
The darkness, the foolishness, the callousness.
No relief in sight. No music. No dancing. No romancing.

To see the other world in this world was always a necessity.
How heavy your feet fell, how heavy each step.
Some days you tried to move. But could not lift your head.
Could not escape those voices. Or even leave your bed.

To see the other world in this world, your sight fixed upon the north star.
You found a light to clear your path, you finally knew your way.
You railed against those who were hopelessly earthbound.
Stepping forward, you took flight. Nothing could hold you back.

Take me with you. Take us with you now.
It's time for all to see the other world in this world.

[Dedicated to Brian F. Saltern]

-Joni Elena Daidone

For Lisa

it felt like
just the other day

we spoke of
new beginnings

the illness you had
seemed a lifetime ago

we did not imagine
it would come back

your condition so fragile
you would soon be gone

now through fragile memories
i weave words of faith

read the *machzor*
for the New Year

see your face
arise from its pages

hear your voice
chant its prayers

another new beginning
the *shofar's* calls to action

the long cries of *tekiot*
the short moans of *shevarim*

the staccato sobs of *teruot*
the final pleas of *tekiot gedolot*

i dip the apple in the honey
add a pinch of salt

-*Rose Bromberg*

In Memory of My Father
- for Charles Everett Kern II (1934-2020)

Make of my head and my heart
nothing more than a little breeze
soft through the crabgrass, lying limp,

not two currents of gale force wind
but one quiet whisper, a whisper
seeking the place you are free.

Make of my bones a dancing puppet
not a frozen mannequin or Punch & Judy
no stasis, no violence, only delight.

Make of my memory a little bowl
not overflowing but just enough:
another moment with the beloved

a grain of rice, enough to fill
an empty spoon, to sustain
a body through loss.

Make of my fingers little fireworks,
dapple the darkness
with blues, maroons, and lavender

little sparks, nothing extravagant,
just enough to show you've been here
and to summon the waterfalls of light
whenever my shadow comes.

-inspired by the 12th century Indian poet Basava

-Alexander Levering Kern

After Life
- for Seymour Solomon (1922-2016)

When my father died, did his soul
free from the confines of his aged body
enter the heavenly tent of Abraham
who welcomes wayfarers and angels?

I can't imagine my father an angel,
not because he was not a good man.
He was. He would be too bored
as an angel.

His soul would be that of a wanderer
dancing the Bronx Lindy-Hop across the stars.
He would never stop watching over us.
My mother, brother and me.

He loved to listen to my Mom's piano, my guitar.
My father did not want my brother to play hockey
on his Lehman College team.
He said "Jewish boys don't play hockey."

My brother, the goalie, once confided that he
was knocked unconscious during a game.
He did not lose teeth so my parents
were none the wiser.

Now there are no secrets from my father.
I can feel his watchful eyes. I thank him
for the night a few days after he died
when the living-room metronome
began to beat a rhythm at 3:am,
to let us know he was here.

-Raquel Solomon

I'll Take Care of It

I visited mom and dad one day on my way from work

Mother sat hunched at the table

Father was standing by the stove

Stirring with a ladle

For sixty years she cooked their meals

A loving wife with flying hands

Never still, until she could no longer stand

He went to minyan on that day and everyday

I had to ask-Why still pray to God each day?

The Nazis killed your family

You spent many years in death camps

How can you still pray?-

"I lived" he said

My mother said

-I doubt that I'll end up

With your father when I die.-

"Don't worry, I'll take care of it," he said

In a tone no one could defy.

His daily prayers echoed acts of kindness.

Now I spy

Mom and Dad together,

Their memory a blessing

As I close my eyes to pray.

-Janet Hiller

Unafraid to Die

for C.R.

Before the year ends,
we gather in your yard
where once you threw yearbooks
into a fire
as if to burn away
memories — bad boyfriends, proms,
your lost brother —

What do your daughters
think watching you through windows
ridding yourself of history
as smoke rises in ribbons
curled across the grass,
brittle and drying in the sun?

What a gift to teach them
we need not carry
the past on our backs,
need not make a homestead
of those paint-peeling rooms,
need not be haunted
by the selves we once were.

Like you, I want to live
unshackled by the threads
of a vintage self,
no longer tied
to last season's fading fabrics
or the wild patterns
that dizzy and disorient.
To return everything
once treasured to ash.

-Magin LaSov Gregg

One moment my life is a stone in me, the next, a star

What I am trying to say is jealousy
does not become me. Yet I am
jealous of those who do not feel
lonely when alone. Once that was me.
Now I am jealous of my recently widowed
friend already invited to Shabbas dinner
by a new beau with white, fly-away
longish hair, good smile, beard scruffy the way
she likes it, while here, I must sink
my tongue into the ice cream of my life,
swim my body through blue water and myriad
friends who come to dine on roasted meats
and warm rolls, and so many calls from well-
wishers, and my brother not surgically challenged
today. One moment my life is a child-
flower made of pastel tissue, (mint green,
butter yellow, shell pink, dusk blue)
held together by an emerald green pipe cleaner,
layers of petals I opened with my fingers,
plush and ancestral, I used to spend hours
unlonely spreading petals into a frightened/
frightening world.

-Doris Ferleger

The human heart

beats 60 to 100 times a minute,
slows down in sleep;
speeds up when anxious, in pain;
changes with our mood,
our exercise pattern,
our comfortability with ourselves.
We take this thumping muscle
for granted, assuming it healthy,
capable. We talk about its
generosity or fear, love or
frustration as though it is something
other, separate from us.
How do we keep our heart
lub-lubbing steadily? What do
we do to care for
our heart and the hearts
of those around us?

-Mary-Lynne Monroe

Self-Preservation During a Pandemic

Two months in, I watched
the TV news reports for the last time.
By then, my worry over contracting COVID
as an ocean churning in a hurricane,
a weight pressing against my chest
and holding me down in bed.
Each morning, I would struggle
to turn off the alarm
and function as if life were the same
even as we were all implored to isolate indoors.

The grim-faced news anchors
weren't much help, either.
Whenever they told me how many people
had tested positive, I would ask,
How many others tested negative?
And whenever they shared how high
the death toll had climbed, I would whisper,
How many of us are still alive?
They never answered, of course,
never listened to me through the thin sheet of glass
that separated us, instead feeding me
facts and figures and other sober details
that tasted of nausea and fear.

I started listening, instead,
to what I knew would bring me peace,
like my heartbeat before a flow of yoga each morning,
poetry podcasts as a side dish to breakfast,
or flute and synthesizer music —
and sometimes birds —
while working from home.

I even heard the soft but deafening voice
in my solar plexus that would scream, *No*,
whenever someone said,
"But it's good to stay informed,
to know how bad it's getting out there."
I'm staying informed, the core of me would say,
since the small dose of headlines
and the next day's weather forecast
were all I could digest.

Had I chosen ignorance?
Was I pretending all the illness and death,
all the loss and sirens and gasping
only a nightmare?
I hope not–
I was only doing
the one thing I could think of
to grab hold of calm amidst the chaos,
to quell the roiling in my head
and let my body sleep
so it could hear what it needed to hear.

-Sara Letourneau

Dreamer

By fifth grade, she knows enough history, knows war is not the answer. She binds herself to John Lennon's "Imagine." She plays it in her room while she's doing homework.

When she's sixteen and still here with us, we tell her it's time to make her Confirmation. She's been in Sunday school since she was little. She's done the work of dragging herself from bed to attend the classes. This is a rite of maturation to accept your faith.

She says she won't do it. She says she doesn't believe. All religion leads to war. I didn't know that at her age. I was fighting my own private battle. I needed my religion. Also, I would never have contradicted my mother.

The Bishop will come and affix his seal of approval. We want her to be just like everybody else. Go to the damn retreat and prepare yourself. You'll get to know the other kids. We got her to promise if she went on the retreat, she could make up her own mind.

What does she do? She goes off and makes a friend who feels the same way about religion and war and fighting. They protest together, go out into the streets on the anniversary of 9-11. They carry signs and wave banners at passing cars going up North Charles Street. *Imagine there's no heaven, nothing to live or die for.*

In her almost empty room hangs a poster with John Lennon's face in profile, wearing his perfectly round glasses. The lyrics to "Imagine" are written in white against a black background. *Imagine all the world living life in peace.* John's war, Vietnam. His song an anthem. *You may say that I'm a dreamer but I'm not the only one.*

She left behind her spray-painted peace signs on the ceiling.

Above us, only sky.

-Christine Higgins

Survival Song

Moods swing and droop like a sky chair
your throat red with embarrassment
you sing a song. No one is looking
but you wish they were.

Walking past humans wondering if a car will lurch
into reverse you count your options: breathe,
name the feeling, ask what evidence you have
for ghosts in the parking lot.

It isn't easy to nail down, like going through a pocket
searching for change and you find lip gloss.
You have options: a trunk of magic
where children pop up dressed like Pantalone

hair all wild, strong smiles on their lips
and they are you. You are a perceptual duality.
I appreciate me, I appreciate me, I miss my dad.
May I be well, may you be well, addressing everyone

who is opening or closing their driver's side door.
For reasons only a teacher can explain I pull
my head back toward the trees, elevate
my neck, relax my shoulders, and sing.

-Bill Ratner

Balm

The longing for happiness,
the burden of its hold
is a deer sprinting unleashed
towards a mirage.

Heartbeats stacked
new on old.
Nothing forgotten.
The past, a breathing corpse.
Love, a flash in the pan.

Shards pricking
the velvet of the heart.
The aloe gel of compassion
enough

to soothe the path of life.

-Vinita Agrawal

Light at the End of the Tunnel

Living in daily depression
Sadness
Loneliness
Felt never ending

This morning,
Determined to change
Made a fearful call
After a long battle,
Got the desired results.

Returned cat food
the 18 year old girls can no longer eat.
Bought special kidney food
Another chore done.

Weather was gloomy
But I wore my new yellow sunglasses
Many people were smiling at me saying
I like your glasses
A homeless woman ran up to me shouting
I want those glasses
So do I
Now becoming cheerful
I continued walking.

As I passed through China town
Stopped at a small fruit and vegetable stand
Countless ladies gathering around to buy goods
I wanted Chinese broccoli and small cucumbers
I said hello to the women in Chinese
"Nee How"
The surprised look on their faces led to

lessons in the Chinese words for all the food
They helped me pick out the best items
I said thank you in Chinese as I left
"Shey Shey"

Walked toward a Japanese restaurant
To order sashimi for lunch and dinner
Talked to the Vietnamese host who made suggestions
We discussed all the fish
He was worrying for me that it wouldn't be ready in time
For me to attend my Spiritual Poetry writing class
He told the kitchen to hurry.
Then he asked me to eat the food and
Write a short poem they could put in the
new menu they were about to print

I left with all my bags
Happy I talked to so many people

Beautiful morning

-Gail H. Kaplan

Your Connection is Unstable

Where is transcendence when all my prayer
songs hollow in the echo of my own voice? My face
a tiny box tiled into a field of boxes, aggregation
of muted congregants, together   separate.

We have lost the cosmic energy of physicality,
the rustle of pants and blouses, the cough,
the occasional sneeze like the exclamation point
of *Amen*; God the power that sizzles
         between our davening bodies.

How can we say: *This is enough*, when connection
leaks through our separate fingers   water scooped
at the edge of a splashing stream, taunting
our dry mouths, our thirsting souls?

Each Shabbat, I bundle this ache to my breast
as I once carried my newborn son, swathed
and sleeping. I want to stroke its shallow philtrum
with my pinkie's tip and whisper:
         I love you. You are not alone.

This *two-week pause* has stretched into
a Sahara, *Hope* a mirage shimmering under
a punishing sun. After too many seasons of drought,
even the cacti grow stunted, craving the caress
         of a small rain.

At night I dream in silk and velvet, trail fingertips
over a braille of connection, palm to palm, your
hand in mine, a duet of breath and touch,
the force of God between us,
         gathering us close.

Essential

We collect them, these things,
      these possessions, held tight.
Then another rises, better perhaps.
Release, grasp again.
Not so valuable after all.

There is comfort and sorrow in this cycle–
Hold, release, empty, fill.
A sister dies.
A child is born.
A love fades.
A step taken.

I travel around the sun.
Plant zinnia seeds, wait for their blooms.
What is essential?
What remains?

Our lives consist of fleeting moments
strung together like pearls of dew on a spider's web,
fragile, shimmering, transient.

Glimpses of beauty, awe.
All is grief and praise.

-Betty Johnson

All the People

who say 'look' and laugh
in astonishment have disappeared. All the people
who make jokes, even bad ones even dad ones
and pun and play word games
have disappeared

behind something behind curtains
or masks, which have 3 layers now,
(a dryer sheet can be used as a middle layer)

All the people
who pick up the half-emptied glass
and say
this glass is half full
and raise a toast to life
l'chaim, chin-chin, a votre sante
have disappeared.   No one here is a bird

or an angel. No one sprouts wings. No one sings
in the street. Everyone carries
a paper bag too full of groceries
too close to their chest, or
their heart.

Everyone is crossing
the street
without looking up. Everyone
watches their device
even if the batteries
flash 1%. Looking for good news. But no one
believes good news.

All the people who say look and laugh
in astonishment
are napping
in the other room. Catching up
on their sleep. Hoping a good nap
will give them fresh eyes.   Wearing a sleep mask or blinders

-Laura Zacharin   75

Gods and Men

The problem with arguing about God
is the problem of logical men
representing rationality
in loud voices and pounding fists
telling me I don't know what I'm talking about
because I'm emotional,
meaning I'm young
and a girl
with long frizzy hair
that won't stay in a ponytail holder,
a girl who can't keep my room clean,
that's why I don't know things.

The problem with arguing about God
is that men sometimes think they're God
because they plan to be rabbis or lawyers,
which is pretty close to God if you're Jewish.
My boyfriend made me read
Maimonides' forty proofs for the existence of God
when I was fifteen,
and we went through each paragraph
line by line, reading about
First Causes and Prime Movers
I got tangled up in the words
and kept having to look up the definitions.
Whatever my boyfriend says is right
because he knows Maimonides
personally, probably.

My boyfriend knows the Shulchan Aruch,
the Code of Jewish Law,
and the prayer after meals
and how many home runs Tom Seaver pitched

and how could I not know who the commissioner of
baseball is.
He's from New York and knows everything,
knows that playing punchball
is as sacred as keeping Shabbat
because men are like God, aren't they
and I just don't get the advanced logic
of baseball stats
and the New Yorker
and an article in Playboy
just for intellectual stimulation.

I read and I listen
and try to make sense of the insensible.
So many years a true believer
until one day I get up from the
cafeteria table,
rise in the middle of a hand of spades,
take my tuna sandwich and my book bag
and say,
You know, I really hate sports.

-Lynda Levy

The Elusivness of What We Seek

The sun large white burning in royal blue.
Clouds gather. A rickety bi-plane writes

messages in the sky for beachgoers: Buy beer,
Vote for a candidate who loves guns

and blows things up. For the moment the clouds
are free of accidents. The new plastics keep

problems contained down under the sea. Overcast
skies tomorrow. We've stopped asking why

bullets tearing into flesh satisfy sociopathic rage.
The smell reminds us of burdens instead of murder.

A toppling village slides down an icy ridge the citizenry
praying to miss the boulders. We don't come

with instruction manuals. I asked an old friend
what he once liked about being an Evangelical.

The rules he said, rubbing his chin.
I liked the rules.

-Bill Ratner

Learning the Metaphors of Peace

The lion and the lamb
have breakfast on the hilltop
after the armies have gone,
eager to share the warmth
of fur and fleece, given
the truth of all they've seen.

The dove sees even more,
above the crushing blows
of whatever battle rages,
the olive branch ready
whenever the tanks
slow on the road.

Embroidered on jean jackets,
hung above our long-lost beds
the three-armed sign of peace
declared we could make love, not war.
Who could have told us then
that we could not change the world?

Yet over and over again,
from the memories of generations,
we pry open defeat
and banish desperation
with the hope that peace
will make its home here. Again.

-Collette Sell

Instructions to Keep the Mind from Going Wild

Do not answer
fire with fire.

Clear as crest
of sea, tell yourself:
you are mine
my darling oh so lonely
one. I tend to you.

Take the Lyft to Newark.
Cease from asking the lover to come
by plane or car or bus or limo.
Spare your heart.

Be made of stone and star
dogwood. Bloom old
bloom old
teacher
the way peace and war teach.

Contain your fires
before they spread beyond
the world.

Tend the wounded
child left behind
there.

Sit with her at the opening
of breath.

Through the world runs
One river, go to the river,
confused or crystal clear,
each molecule awakening.

-Doris Ferleger

The Last Quarter of the Pie

The pie is three quarters eaten,
What is left is full of rich dark fruit,
Henna haired grandchildren,
ripe friendships, honeyed with age,
and the promise of what new buds will yield.

I have eaten of the product of blossoms,
The rich dark cherries of young love and long marriage,
the bitter mincemeat of grief and loss, and
the comfort of cream offered by friends

My plate, balanced with bitter greens, red berries,
almost consumed now, I am ready for the rich dessert.

-Marilyn Mohr

THOUGHTS FROM ONE OF OUR POETS

What is a Spiritual Poem?

Behind a spiritual poem is the unified connection to a source that never began and never ends. This eternal presence exists before any words flow and feels like the vehicle for awakening inspiration. Receiving a poem from this vast untouchable well moves an electric bolt through the body; it bypasses the mind and opens the heart to the very fabric of this creative force. Anyone who has felt it, knows it. There is no forgetting it. Any poem that touches you in this way, electrifying your body, your being and opening perception beyond the mind and senses is a spiritual poem and stays with you like a lover's eyes, seeing something beyond what is there. It may not be the same poem for any two people. What awakens us to this vast resource is a mystery, but often, it comes with wings of beauty, a felt sense of awe and deeper knowing that rests someplace we may not usually perceive. I do not write spiritual poetry; it writes itself through me. And it is feeling this true writer's voice that makes a poem feel like spiritual poetry when I read it.

-Cit Ananda

The Struggling Vine is Not a Metaphor

for hope or perseverance. Come, sit.
We already drill enough for oil. Nature
must not exist to serve

    our stories of heartache. Watch the lake
for itself, the calm and rot and buds crunched
underfoot. The water mirrors only sky;

    why insist on a crystal ball? The moonlight flows
because it does. The river ripples because it must.
And what is more storyless than the wind

    sometimes silent, sometimes squalling
unlanguaged and therefore, free? The mud-root
lotus offers no lessons to inhale, no shortcuts

    that balsam a guide, a shield, a guarantee.
Drink your to-go latte and feel the bronze
rappelling down your throat. Sunbathe

    in this moment of a star living out its long-
short youth. Ache, moral-free. Scream into aloof
air. Sing, when you're done, like only you can.

    That is enough.

-Pervin Saket

Vow

I vow to cling to peace
when war beckons
with every new headline
I vow to set the table
and respect the meal
even when I'm alone
I vow to return phone calls
I'd rather avoid
I vow to live in the world of neighbors
waving from their driveways
strangers who need my recognition
I see you, you exist
Here we are
living on the same street
I vow to drive safely
watch for children on bicycles
and stray cats who shouldn't be procreating
but are
I vow to take a breath
look you in the eye
take a dollar out of my purse
before I drive on

-Lynda Levy

Bread and Strangers

Mingling in congregations of unnamed faces,
I have chased God through many doors,

taught at my mother's empty breast
that hunger is a testament to faith. In this time

of pandemic, I am, again, a wandering Jew,
leapfrogging from Zoom to Zoom,

cyberspace surveillant of *Mishpacha*
from sunset beaches to Rocky Mountains

to New York's crowded chanting in unsynced
melodies. I've lost all sense of home. I join a group

of loosely braided strangers near lifeguard station 23
for *Tashlich*. In masks and non-latex disposable

gloves, we gather empty bottles, cigarette butts,
a used condom, a lonely red toy shovel

as our *Tikkun Olam*. If only it were that easy
to heal the world. Seven people, fourteen hands

and miles of sand we will never touch. *Don't
think*, I tell myself, *of the islands of plastic*

clogging the arteries of the sea. We fill
a grocery bag as we march from parking lot

to surf. I burrow my feet into wet sand.
Ground myself. Is God here? I squint

into the sun's reproach splintering the waves,
sunder the day-old roll I bought to serve

as my modern-day *Azazel*. What rituals
we have conceived to relieve the chafing

weight of all our daily failures. Every tower
I build undone by tide. And yet, each day I wake

to feed the cat and weekly shop for two fragile neighbors
who wipe down every egg, apple, milk jug, pickle jar.

Now, I reach into my bag, cast a fistful of bread
into the waters to expunge my sins.

The seagulls shrill a chorus of gratitude
as they tussle over crusts and crumbs.

Originally published in Sheila-Na-Gig online September 2021

-Elya Braden

There Is Only One Question

It is not how much
do you want to live?

But how much do you want
to love?

It is a question you already
know the answer to

clenched in your blue heart's fist
when the doctor is explaining

how long the treatment will take
and that it's a lot like getting

the flu every three weeks.
So you resolve

to stay miserable
every damn day of your life

for a year
so that you'll be able to fall in love

every week for the rest:
To love chocolate and lipstick

and soft knitted caps
made by church ladies

you've never met.
To love your hair

when you greet it again
and bald men with beards

deliciously rough
on your parched lips.

There's a world of 10,000 things to love.
And you know you want to.

Of that, there is no question.

–Beth Walker

What Brings Me to God

What brings me to God
Is color, now as the
world explodes in harvest hues.
The yellow beckons me, on its
way to pure gold.

What brings me to God
is family, as flawed and
imperfect as any group.
They are mine,
God's offering, personified.

What brings me to God
is panic, and a litany
of prayers that spring
unbidden from my lips
to God's ears.

What brings me to God
is song, from Morissette to Mozart,
to Lydia- my grandmother
who sang hymns
as she worked.

-Leah C. Mueller

So Much is Flammable

transitory, lost, ash to wind.
I burn. I desire an end
to burning, to be quiet cinders.
But to have light requires heat;
to have love needs passion,
even if in a platonic manner.

Surrender to flame is difficult.

Could I let fire sear away
that which is finished
and no longer serves?
Could I be swept clean
in the brilliant New Year Light?
Could I give over
my own stubborn will
and yield to Spirit, be cleaved
by its incandescent, kind sword,
and opened to the gifts of angels?

Then, perhaps, peace would unfurl
from within, where it hides, nascent,
and I would cease to resent what is
because it is arduous and unrelenting.
I would let go, at last surrender.
If not as I wish, still
all manner of things will be well.

-J.M.R. Harrison

How to Quench a Thirsty Soul

*After Kabir - **I Said to the Wanting Creature Inside Me**,*
"Do you believe there is some place that will make the soul less thirsty?"

The passage is a narrow gate with two paths —

one within; the other, without.

You will find the place to quench your soul's thirst,

satisfy its parched yearnings;

still the fathomless gush of groans;

flood its corridors, water its wanting chambers.

Within the gate are thresholds, doors;

listen; walk toward one;

connect to a landscape of possibilities,

here and there, close up; away,

There is not one single place

to satiate one's parched soul.

to fill it up, replenish.

There are many.

Don't expect smooth edges. Each choice will bring potholes,

thistles or blisters. Accept imperfections.

Walk in anyway, whether you are dismissed or

disregarded. You will find your bliss

within the world's great need.

Look for it.

Your outward journey will replenish the inward.

Hear the call when it coos;

What you choose may be unfamiliar,

outside your comfort zone;

paddle, peregrinate.

Press on toward the mark of your upward calling. *Phil 3: 13-14*

You will quench your thirsty soul.

-Lynda Rush Myers

Follow Your Heart

Follow your heart
Through our
Similar rituals
And love will appear
Through the sacred
Incense
"Ketoret"
In the lighting of candles
"Or".
To
Mondays and Thursdays
When the Torah is read
And Muslims fast
And
The Christian communion of wine and wafer
To the Jewish
Challah and Wine on Shabbat
Can you see
The love connecting
Us all?
Can you hear us all calling out loudly?
The Shofar
The Muezzin
The Church bells
Cry out
LISTEN!
Follow your heart.

-Tammy Einstein

Happiness

Every imagined happiness is conditioned
by desire and expectation.
Do not be bound by these.

Acceptance of all that is
will take you where you want to go.
After all, everything led to this moment.

All the forces of the universe.
All your choices.
All the gifts you were given, all the trials.

Everything is in motion.
The start of your journey here
was the end of another in the womb.
Do not fear, love.

The end of your journey here
is the beginning of another there
in realms unimaginable.

To be happy
expect not, want not.
Just be, love.

-Kay Allgood

Only the Body Can Dance

In the back room or the basement or a shed
that no one's opened up in years, the lock corroded,
we have to break the lock to get inside–
someone is teaching your body to dance. It sounds like dance
or a song you once recognized. Someone is teaching you
the language of optimism or a prayer, to say grace,
a benediction. Someone teaches you hope. Teaches your body
to dance. And it sounds like this. Someone unlocked
a door. A door you couldn't see before it was unlocked. A door
you'd forgotten, blended into a background you got so used to
you couldn't see a door. Someone is playing
your favorite song. From that time when. Someone is singing
or you hear music in your head. Or you're humming
or someone is playing guitar so quietly it's hard to know for sure
that it's guitar. But you recognize the song. From that time when.
Someone broke the lock on a locked-up door. Says left foot first
then right. A beat vibrates in the earth
beneath you. The music is playing, the earth is humming.
In the dark, in a room you barely recognize, a body
that's your body, is learning how to dance.

-*Laura Zacharin*

The beginning of happiness

Happiness begins with music wrapping my ears
as C and D minor make an appearance.

The feel of a great song makes me want to
elongate my arms extend my fingers till
they reach the moon as I close my eyes.

Music visits my body, and it makes my body
sing the song of the high C and the 5, 6, 7
and then start again with the 1, 2, 3, for
a new beginning.

Dance it off!
Dance it all!

That's where my heart meets the sun,
through the music of invitation,
through the music of remembrance,
through the music of embracing
it all today.

-Gabriela Iñiguez

Waiting for Sound

Sitting in this room hooked up to
a writing workshop
by bandwidth and ear phones,
nothing comes.

An indecisive day
outside this ground floor window
not terribly cloudy
humidity low, hugging the air.

This room furnished
with closets and drawers,
shelves and chests,
all of which hold things:
pictures and books, memory.

This room filled with quiet for now
until the phone rings,
or a garbage truck arrives,
or the twin boys next door get out
of virtual school and dribble and dunk.

This room filled with waiting.

What next after a book
I carried for thirteen years
now published?

What next at this writing desk —
this life —
but to breathe,
accept the empty,
to wait for sound.

-Maria Giura

White Peony Poems

Poetry dawns with morning's first sip
of White Peony tea. Its subtle courage

warms hands that cling to mug
distills pen's yearning, condenses it to words.

Tea lifts them skyward astride its steam
to fill the wispiest of clouds. These float

and shield from sun's daggers, water
monkeyflower with wisdom and wit, dispatch

winds to carefully wear away walls
built to keep poetry out.

-Nancy K. Jentsch

Word

Words reflect the recesses of the soul.
May you be mindful of your thoughts there.
For thoughts become words,
become sentences,
become motives,
become actions.
May you strive that your actions
become beautiful prayers.

The point of words starts with a dot,
becomes a line,
becomes a shape,
becomes a letter,
becomes a word.
And the point of words
is the silence from whence they began.

The point of words is communion
with oneself,
with ones origin,
with each other.
In the beginning was the Word,
the Primal Will manifest.

-Kay Allgood

Start With a Question Mark

At the end of the first
sentence of the year,
a perfect piece of punctuation,
its soft back resembling a camel
riding into the desert, a hundred
aching miles without a sip of water.

A question mark is not
a closed door, like a period
or semicolon, not boring
like a comma — too easy
to misspell as *coma* —
not accusing like a dash.

A question mark's top curve
swerves like an open road
hemmed by fallow fields
where everything
might grow, where the air
is still and earnest
as a child bending
down in prayer.

-Magin LaSov Gregg

Although

the world has gone insane — think of Van Gogh
who loved to make beautiful things, and Rothko
who said, "Make every picture miraculous."
It was Osip Mandelstam — reciting his poems
from memory, as he lavished the world
with his lyric poems, in spite of the knocking
at his door, in spite of betrayals. Dickinson
with her rapture in living, Shelley, cheering
like a nightingale in the dark. I tape poems
to the walls of my rooms like paint chips —
shades of pomegranate, turquoise powder,
robin's egg, mystic blue, — someone once said,
the artist lives inside the art.

-Deborah Gerrish

On Making Poems

It is an itch just at that spot
on the right scapula where your left
index finger strains to scratch,
driving you to squat and glide
your back against the molding
of the nearest jamb, an answer
to the urge, a cow given over
to suckle.

It is a riddle in search of retort,
allegory, pun. It unveils clues
and extends metaphors en route
to Pandora's box for the curious.

It is a fuse primed in my gut
or my brain. It inspires outings
down rabbit holes named Webster
or Wikipedia, where the last piece
of the puzzle finds its place and bows
are sometimes tied up pretty.

I take up my pen like a match, pray
for kindling. I enter fallow fields
or greener pastures, sit at tables set
in the presence of my inner critics.
I scribble, erase, doodle, pause,
curse the god who abandons me,
though I lack nothing but the perfect
words in the right order.

-Pamela Wax

Out of a Great Need You Must Go Now

But first empty your cup and wash it.
Place your shoes by the bed.

Wake up from this dream
and declutter your dusty delusions

like clearing out the house after a long sickness.
You will cling to many possessions

but they have never been yours to keep.
Not even the shoes. Not even the cup.

Go naked. Take nothing
when you leave this house of longing.

All those jewels you have sewn
into the hems of your ragged clothes

are just weighing down your ragged soul.

-Beth Walker

Soft Words

You can use my soft words as a cushion for your head ~Hafiz

my loves
use my soft words
as solace

> to bind your wounds
> when angry clubs
> break your skin

> to make a bed
> for the stray dog
> you carry home tonight

> to swaddle the baby
> of the woman lost
> near the border

use these words
to beat your heart
on a frigid and broke morning

> to soothe the ache
> as you wake
> from heroin dreams

                         to feed your soul
                         like new wine
                         in old skins

let my words weave
a tapestry of
your almost-lost memories

               draw a map
               between your desire
               and my offerings

                         let these words shine
                         long after you and I
                         have joined Hafiz

                         on the pillow of his poetry

                         -Joanell Serra

Everywhere Duty, Beauty

I slept and dreamt that Life was Beauty,
I woke and found that Life was Duty.
Ellen Sturgis Hooper

Everywhere there is drudgery. The day a blur of chores.

Laundry into the washer first thing, and last thing at night
      out among stars pinned to the sky
    I pull clothes pegs from frozen sheets.

If I can't take a moment here
— at the end of this day, with my deep desire for rest —
    to pause and look up
      then Duty, which can shoulder all else aside
    has no grander purpose. Or I do not comprehend it.

Because the Divine follows me everywhere —
      along the trail of strawberries through the overgrown flower bed
      among the rhododendrons, poppies and columbines —
        my eyes, my mouth savor such sweetness.

Surely, in the midst of picking fruit and pulling weeds
    Spirit is just ahead and behind me
harvesting   hoeing   easing my tasks
    everywhere seeding Beauty in the midst of Duty.

-Janice Lore

Tashlich

I enter this new year —
seek the stillness,
stand before the silver
foamy froth of sea,
wish for a year
inscribed with peace.

I toss my piece of bread
into the waves —
a symbol to release
my sins and sorrows
with hope for forgiveness
and to start anew.

As the waves
rise and fall,
I toss in another piece
and wish for strength.

Guided by words from
the Old Testament,
I cast my bread
upon the waters,
my spiritual renewal
its own reward.

-Rose Bromberg

I Want

To wake with a full spirit, greet the promise
of new beginnings, believe I can

climb mountains, even if only
made from concrete. I will stand

on the highest terrace, sing my joy
at the sirens and passing traffic.

Scaring pigeons, I will howl my truth
at the sky and his 27 companions.

Bathe daily in the ecstasy of being. I want
to sleep each night with this promise

beating within me, daring to dream
then - I want to awaken.

-Nitya Nedyam

Holy Dishes

the pot is slippery in my hand
as water pipes through plumbing
from the river, through the water main

filtered by public works,
heated so sweetly
by water heater and electricity

in our own unique blend of solar and utility power
it's drinkable, you know,
the water, that is, not the solar power

my hands squish through soap
purchased from the store,
shipped to shelves by workers unknown

made in a factory employing thousands
placed in plastic, oh the plastic,
extracted, refined, everlasting polymers

the green gel inside
with just the right amount
of froth and bubble

I wanted the bio-based one,
but my husband didn't like the suds
and so, compromise

yes to soap, no to dish soap
and so it goes
the dishes, the washing, the compromise

and the sponge, let's not forget the sponge,
made from wood or more plastic
to exaggerate luscious lather

the elbow grease, of course
for there were small scorches
from the meal cooked with care

how holy to clean dishes
where you can't recognize
that anything was ever in them

the pot sits now, empty,
a blank canvas
awaiting the next creation

-Sharon Neubauer

What Can a Human Being Offer to God?

Inspired by Lalla

I wanted to be a nun,
not for the white wimple, but for silence.
Then a monk, not for saffron robes,
but to be empty of everything but God
or Love which is the same thing.

Skin still soft from the womb,
eyes grave with questions,
I gave myself away. Fast as a blink.
Before my fingers curled
to grasp the yellow day.

I was born to abandon myself.
It doesn't matter if the child
flies into the future on butterfly wings
or falls into alchemy when buttoning her coat.
She is gone. As gone as I am.

A calling and an answer,
holy as a first breath.
Seeking follows emptiness.
But truth also lies in this:
emptiness follows seeking.

Now I have spent a lifetime
in the alteration of vastness.
A tuck here, a stitch there,
to make the moon-beaded gown of infinity
fit the body of painstaking possibility.

I offer the moon dress to the Spirit,
offer songs to the Singer,
offer knowing to the Unknown,
frantic acts of penance
in the hours that remain.

Until today. When the grave-eyed child
shakes dandelion seeds from her shoulders
stops me with a saffron wave and says,
"The Spirit does not require sacrifice.
Gratitude is enough to offer God."

-Collette Sell

Tonglen
(After the Tibetan Buddhist Breathing Meditation)

Awake too early in the day
my mind is still a cloud.
Beyond my window, outstretched arms
of Grandmother Oak
are limned with vestal robe.
The snow still falls
but by now has lost its faith.
I try to breathe its gentle rhythm
but snow is only exhalation.
There's no inbreath to come.

Which comes first:
breathing out or breathing in?

I am a tonglen
a returning spiral
carved in timeless Celtic shrines.
I go into the world
into you as far as I can.
I send my love out fully
like an outbreath to its end
and hold myself empty
a beat.
Two.
Am *there*.
Until the turning the returning
when things always change.

Like the tide sucks the sea
back home again
like the sky grabs back earth's wetness
holding it in mist and fists of cloud.
Which one owns the water –
puddle or air?
Which one only borrows –
updraft or downpour?
Does the shore absorb the nearest sea?
Does the sea pack souvenir sands?
At night they dance inside each other
intermingle, course through, and return.
You can't tell where one ends
and the other begins.

                    Which comes first:
                    breathing in or breathing out?

            I breathe in the world
         and all you have to offer
              how you suffer
              how you hate.
          I take you into me
     surround you with my flesh
        carry you in my blood
    dissolve your prickly crystals
    sew up your broken promises
            hold you *here*
    until again it's time to turn.

Wind carries me away
and can carry me back.
A river flows but also eddies
forming its own spirals.
It sheds its silt
and grows a delta.
Inter-tidal creatures
live both in drought and flood.
But snow only seems to fall
too tired to engage
too unbalanced
to forgive
to try again.

Which comes first:
breathing out or breathing in?

There is no beginning
only going on
in and back out
out and back in
rocking back and forth on the porch
swaying in a slow dance
a song sung in a round
voices spiraling
our scents interweaving

In my dream
my life is a tonglen meditation,
breathing your need
all the way into my red live lungs
my limbs my mind
and sending out a tide of transformed meaning
to all the shores
where someone needs it back.

-Molly Howes

115

There are lots of ways to be impoverished

Sister Miriam would say, when I'd scorn
the classy zip codes, the posh trappings
of the clients who entered my office to be heard.
I became echo, container, confessor, advocate
for devils and angels. Sometimes I thought to swap
out her faith and her vows to feed the hungry
campers in cardboard on Broadway, begging
to be seen. Yes, she'd say, *some of them can pay
a pretty penny for the food you offer,* when I told
her about the man who paid me triple my fee,
the man who lost his wife. I made my peace
ladling comfort for thirsty souls, while I looked
down upon the streets at my bare feet, my growling
gut, wondering at my own hiding ways.

-Pamela Wax

The World

A river of discrete moments
discrete beings
all floating together
until there is only
one temple.

-Lynn Palumbo

One With All

I am Home.
There is no seeking.
Life is the blessing.
Now is the vine
dripping with nectar
radiant as crystal dew
adorning earth's lean, green children
rising as they do
when the dawn of day
sparks her inner pulse
with infinite grace and brilliant light.

I find myself in the dew.
Wrapped in night's embrace
enveloped in a blade of grass
gently revealed in morning's light
by the sweet, slow reach
of the sun's outstretched arms
licking the grass blade open
with soft fingers of fire,
carrying the right warmth
to wiggle the hydrostatic sphere of my bubble.

I am wiggling in the light,
I am nuzzled in the darkness
I am as cozy in the cupped arm of the blade
as the warm touch of the flame.
I am Home.

-Cit Ananda

And Then the Green of the Leaves

And then the green   of the leaves

            calls out   silence inside

the ear   rings out   a blue cavern of sky

        sings out

          while a priestess chants

a song   heard by women   around

the world   they step to the left   step to the right.

      Land your staff into red fertile   earth & bleed

    the world is a   drum humming

a heartbeat of celebration.

       Whose child are you?

Do you believe you are born from the white-hot center

    of the un-known

    where your true name

    whispers as you first   open

       your eyes–beloved beloved

-*Alicia Elkort*

After Hafiz, "We Should Talk About this Problem"

I have fallen in love with Someone
Who hides inside you.

Who (or What) is the *Someone* hidden
inside? Your shape unknown, unnamed.

Not circle nor star. I cannot find
your eyes or mouth, but hear you, now

and then, a kind of singsong in-
tongues, but not tongues, rather air's

molecules transforming
into the language of mercy.

Are you Mercy?
A midrash transforming plain text?

The Selichot I could not learn by heart?
Not scholar, not singer, not air or dust though almost—

I know you are there, always have been, waiting
for me to find you, us.

-Amy Small-McKinney

What I Want to Say Is . . .

...I have tried my best.
Well, some times more than others.
Okay, maybe a few times not at all, but
when I have tried my best
it is because I simply showed up—
again and again—
at the courthouse, food bank, bedside,
picket line, celebration, rally
when I knew what to do
or hadn't a clue,
on good hair days and bad and
I got out of the way—

let You
love my neighbor,
challenge the Pharisees,
welcome the stranger through my Upstate accent,

let You
shine through my aging eyes,
comfort through my arthritic hands,
listen to the ones who are never heard,

let You
choose the song,
lead the dance,
break the bread—
and what I really want to say is
thank You.

-Susan Whelehan

121

Now is the time

- after Hafiz

Now is the time for the world to know
the infinite spaces between you and me,
elegant in their energy, one pulse
and I'm nearer than breath.

Now is the time for the world to see
desire ripening as a plum,
scattered sunlight across the table,
lit from ten thousand stars.

Between the world and me the senses stand
as friends saluting the beauty of day,
or sea sponges absorbing each passing moment
as pure gift – rhyme not reason, embracing

the deeds of the ancestors:
they are listening at the cellar door
in wintertime when the harvest is done
when the scent of apples invites you, Come

abide with me, when evening slips
its golden kerchief over the mountains
and mourning doves sing, Abide with us,
oh evening song, vesper, compline, shore of night

I will never leave you to face your fears alone.

-Alexander Levering Kern

122

How God Filters In

My study is dark
like a theater before the opening act.
I like it that way.
Pen in hand, a clean page,
I wait.

And, if my timing is just right,
God filters in through the venetian blinds.

I wouldn't dare pull the cord
to let in more.
The brightness would blind me.
The orange glow would absorb me,
turning my body weightless and thin
until it evaporated from the heat.

No, the strips of light that illuminate my hands,
the chair, the rug,
are enough.

I will still stumble from my room
and down the stairs,
waving my journal like stone tablets,
with no one to convince
but myself.

-Terry Davis

Why Not?

Why worry about whether the bush
was literally on fire,
or whether the story was only metaphorical?

Why hypothesize that it might have just
seemed to blaze because its fiery autumn leaves
were seen and recounted by an aging leader with blurred vision?

Why not simply accept that a miracle occurred,
an unprecedented event that defied logic and experience,
requiring faith for validation?

Why not? is the verbal equivalent of outstretched, open palms,
poised for awe to land upon them like a glistening bubble,
and to be grasped with tender reverence.

-Susan L. Lipson

The Truth

The Truth plays in the band,
deep in the band, with his flute,
his miracle flute, or maybe it's his tuba,
something golden and round at the end
of which is a giant ear or mouth or tunnel.

Or maybe she, the Truth, is off tying
her shoe, wearing something pink
and taffeta and back-lit.

Or maybe the Truth is driving
a truck...the truck that brought the band
in the first place, a flatbed truck with bags
of sawdust and a California plate XY235H.

Or, perhaps, the sawdust is the Truth,
wanting nothing, hoping for nothing,
or the band uniforms, with their gold buttons
and the epaulets and braid or the sound
of the feet, not the boots, but the actual feet
in the socks, in the boots, or the audience.

Maybe the Truth is the place where the audience
was once born years ago...the audience looking now
with one eye, one heart, one mind, one finger,
ten toes, two ears, one sky with a sun in it—
a white sun round as a hole, floating like a ball
in a nameless black space, except for itself.
So, we orbit the Truth and feel its pull inward
and upward as we spin or turn.

I think it's the girl, though, next to
the garbage cans below the bleachers
at the back but within earshot of the band.
That's the Truth: the way she stares
from the shadows and blinks at the open light
while the music moves over her like a scarf.
The round metal can waiting for a sort of Thursday,
waiting to be emptied. The Truth wishing always
        to be emptied.

                                    -*Jon Pearson*

Falling Apart

The world needs me to fall apart
to let the pieces of this glued-together vessel
crumble and shatter
like ancient jugs
once used for water,
now in shards,
littered across bedrock and time
bringing reminders and slivers of color,
drawn as brown on clay,
to their eons-old resting place.

The world needs me to fall apart
to crumble and shatter
into ancient cracks,
well hidden,
once blocked from view
littered through the lineage
slashed into being
surviving the march inward of oppression
the knock on the door
by gorgeous, blue-eyed, angelic, chiseled-jaw lads
seeking targets for extermination,
old hooks, crystalized into hard residue.

The world needs me to fall apart
even as I hold the door tightly,
knuckles fisted,
securing it shut that I may possibly
fool time
with the desire to hold it together
carry the water
look the part
play the role and perform on task.

The world needs me to fall apart.
I resist,
compelled by custom,
the rules of the game
learned so well
to avoid creating more discourse.
I resist
or maybe hide from sight,
from a desire to feel something other than pain,
the tearing apart of memories,
not just my memories,
but ancient remembrances
vessels for muddy water
shards in the body
frozen crystals of hatred
anchored into depths,
unfathomable and dreary
a form of concealment,
layered in watery towers,
that spill awkwardly everywhere
fluidly sliming the entirety of the life -
deluge.

But only if I fall apart.

After the flood, there is only Light.

-Cit Ananda`

Elusive

The answer is here, somewhere. I know this
to be true, yet I can't hear it or see it.

I wait, weep, wonder and wander,
still, nothing. Will it come at night?

Will it speak to me in a dream?
Will I know what to listen for? or

Will my spilled thoughts deepen the silence, my
hopes empty into a world of my own making?

Perhaps. Perhaps not. My mind cluttered with
too many questions, but no clarity, elusive.

The answer is here, somewhere.
I just need to be quiet, and wait.

-Ricki Aiello

Even When

Even when I didn't keep faith
with the poems,
the poems kept faith with me.
They waited in maternity wings
while babies nursed,
as the children grew;
they waited by swing sets,
in the doctor's office,
in the laundry room
and the garden beds;
the invisible patience of poems.
They waited by the moving van
as packing crates were lifted
and loaded,
on the ocean liner,
and all during the war.
While chicken roasted,
while broccoli steamed, as the rice-pot
over-boiled. When the siren sounded,
as the ambulance arrived,
the poems kept their waiting.
January's drifting snow
and bitter wind
that somehow turned to June...
and all the while the poems knew.

-Susan Jackson

Psalm 151

Adoshem, are You one with us? Does it hinge on our

Belief in You? Are You not unknowable? Is it enough how

Chazal guides us? Must we only know You through mortals? How

Desperate we constantly are for Your greatness, Your presence.

Every sign of You seems to be shadowed by this world's horror.

Fain, we would do with much less of that to settle our doubt in You.

God, we do not deny Your everlasting majesty. But from Your silence

How are we to recognize Your compassion? Our sages sat in darkened rooms

Inebriated with the idea of You, in the comfort of prayers and argument.

Just men, they were, who knit a thousand years and more of suffering together.

Kindred spirit, HaShem, ruler of the bright green earth, the iridescent sky of blue,

Long, empty distances of grey-blue ocean, babbling brooks, extraordinary creatures,

May Your glory be repeated forever and ever. But so too, should You have responsibilities.

Never to speak to us, why not? But if not, why not instead make this world a better place?

Overcome Your reluctance. Our people are desperate. Here we are completing, in

Poetry, biology, chemistry and physics, Your every thought. We don't need the Grand Design.

Quite the opposite, we need Your love in concrete terms: less unnecessary death,

Rivers of freedom from fear, an end to slavery, an exaltation of truth, an end to our

Suffering. And we must too, do our part, as it says, na-aseh v'nismah. We want to

Trust You. We are ready to be baalei teshuva. To work with You in this joint enterprise.

Uberty for all is the vision we think we share with You. And still we recognize our own

Vulnerability. All the generations of humankind have felt Your mellifluous love. Send

Word that You are with us. And not just to us, but for the sake of Your Holiness teach us

Xenophilia that we might live in respect and peace with all Your creatures in this world.

Yielding to us on this small point, we promise not to wish for more and more. Let not

Zealotry overtake us. Our desire is to live in Your honor and for Your glory.

-Simon Constam

Mirror, Mirror

Not the one
that reveals the future or scans the kingdom
for the fairest, nor the one

hazy with age and marred with hairlines,
its silver back flaking.
But the one Hadewijch saw, that waits

within until you seek it,
its only task to reflect the light-
shine of your unclouded face.

-Karen Luke Jackson

What We Leave Behind

Not the Pietà —
   the crucified Christ's body held
      by the marble folds of his mother's lap.

Not the Suez Canal —
   the parting of dry land
      opening passage through the Red Sea.

Not the symphony's scribbled score.

Instead, notes swelling from discarded staves.
   Freed from their assigned symbols, they strum the air.

Not the flame but the flicker.

In the moment of guttering
   we become wax — softened, malleable.
   A wisp of smoke from the spent wick.

-Janice Lore

Remembering the Quiet Mystery

What if God simply changed his mind
and called off the explosion
of love that burst into light
before there was a before

or an atom or electron
before particles and shooting stars
before black holes and dark matter
before Orion and the constellations
and the seven moons of Jupiter
emerged from the celestial soup

before galaxies began their trip to infinity
before the universe
played midwife to her infant earth
before wind carved canyons
out of rock and the rock
bequeathed water like liquid grace
before gills and wings and lungs

before the dinosaur and the slow eyed doe
that even now is peering through my window
before the cardinal in the balsam
the butterfly and the fruit fly
before Queen Anne's Lace and onion grass
before the alphabet and the pen
longing for paper and the paper
longing for the word

before my delft bowl and the pears that fill it
before the chestnut tree that gifted me
a host of sturdy shelves that even now
bear witness with photographs
to my one and only sentient life

it was all there
folded into that first love
bubbling in the primal explosion
asking nothing more of us than to love
everything that God loves
every rock every fish every star
including you, including me.

                                        -Marion Goldstein

What I Am Not Able To Tell

A day like any day,
me at my desk,
immersed in words.
Then something began to move,
out there... in me,
like a cloud dispersing
or the beat
of the hummingbird's wing
so fast
like the whole world
opening up
and I can only say, well,
everything,
everything revealed the divine:
wood gleamed, the four legs
the writing table, windows and walls,
the floor itself... I wandered into the hall and
down the stairs — was the kitchen holy too?
The sack of potatoes with dirt from the earth,
the can with trash waiting to go to the bin outside...
impossible, but it too glowed with holiness,
as if a monk had risen out of his cave
and walked forward in blessing to light the candles
on an altar there in my kitchen.
I did not fall to my knees.
I did not know what to do
with such profusion, the divine
everywhere I looked, in everything
I touched. So one by one
I lifted each potato
and washed the nubby skin
in the cold, clear water,
dried my hands
with the linen cloth,
lit the stove,
and began to hum.

-Susan Jackson

Neither Silver nor Gold

Watermark me, O Love.

Imprint, stamp your character.

Hold in brightness,

ink in presence indelible,

clear

in the heart of currency.

Exchange me.

Circulate our fibers,

yourself embedded

to avoid all counterfeit.

Beyond a secure vault

redeem me one last time

in your repository.

-Thelma Wurzelbacher

Unnumbered Names for God

It does not matter in the least.
You can call God "Fred" or "Flora"
or even "Fido," and she will listen,
offer presence, be companion.

Lift up your heart like a cup.
Drink deep. She will fill it.
Taste freedom
from all dread and drudgery.

She sings a lullaby —
one you half-remember.
Heart wounds that cry out
for balm find surcease.

Let Fred comfort you.
Let Flora soothe bitter memory
and ease your buried griefs.
Dwell in Fido's perfect peace.

-J.M.R. Harrison

In Dreams

One foot planted on a cliff,
the other foot on another cliff,
straddling the river,
a deep ravine.
Strength, power,
awe fill my belly.
I have a view of people
walking paths, rafting,
staring down from clifftops.
I am Divine, in love
with this creation.
A raft overturns, spilling
contents into whitewater.
Poking my finger into the river,
the current slows,
people stutter from the water.
They do not thank me
for my help. No matter.
My heart is sated.

-Mary-Lynne Monroe

Open the Door

Look within,
deep within
and we will find
Divine
standing, waiting
for us to open the
Door of our Heart
and welcome in
That Which Was
always within,
and our loneliness
will vanish.
For we are never alone
when we listen
to That Voice
speaking softly
within – waiting
for each of us.

-Duane L. Herrmann

When

When the inside/outside world speaks to me
I hear in a language not of words

Even, during a moment of my own incredible happiness,
Like when I am trading faces with an 18-month-old,
I can be suddenly lost in its fullness

And later, if you ask, I will tell you
Of being momentarily overtaken by
Immensity

-Shelley Rio-Glick

Moving Bricks

A love so deep
so formidable
in every breath

that it leaves you
cradling the intent
ingrained in cosmic design.

Often overall quiet,
we are constantly moving the bricks
in destiny's drama.

Sliding this way and that
in poignant and moving spirit
building a circle of neat homes.

Bargaining integral things
 just to know the inner sap
of all the trees in the world.

Mapping out blueprints
for the Great Escape
the route of which is not known.

Being here, doing what we need to do
through our filament of Light
the mind fells great oak trees of time with a golden knife.

This self-mastery over falling
acquired over many lifetime
is the point - the tireless pursuit of arriving.

-Vinita Agrawal

Tompkins Square Park Pastoral

The lone tree at the edge of Avenue A and 7th street
dropped its leaves into Tompkins Square Park.
The man sitting across from my park bench
stood up and smiled.

He then gathered leaves and returned to me.
"I will give you some leaves and they might bring
you what you are wishing for.

Adam and Eve lived here years ago.
See that 3rd floor garden apartment on 7th
between A & B?" He pointed to the window.

"The neighborhood gentrified and they were priced out.
The Tree of Life was cut down years ago.
The Tree of Knowledge of Good and Evil
split in a hurricane. Good and Evil spread everywhere.

Now the trees here are just like any other but they are merciful
too. They take in carbon dioxide and give out oxygen.
That is the life's work of the tree."

He asked me "What are you writing on your pad?"
I said "I am writing a pastoral poem.
Perhaps I should include a speaker."

He said, "I will be honored to be your speaker.
Do you know how many poems, paintings
and short stories I have tried to enter in this park?"

He said, "Here on earth we labor and carry time
that thief on our backs. Don't forget to look
at the trees and the night sky."

I said thank you as he walked away.
I looked at the stars in the night sky
above the lamplight..

-*Raquel Solomon*

The Tin Altar

Crows large as chickens
migrate from their hiding places
deep in the arms of birch and maple

they are waiting for the neighbor woman
the one who cannot find
her mind, who no longer knows
her children, her husband, her kitchen

only the feral cats who await amidst
the bamboo stalks for her morning ritual.

Her alter is a tin table
where she places her bucket
of fresh water and wet food
then kneels, as though in prayer,
but no, she is extracting a dish
of stagnant water from a plastic
cat shelter near the yard's perimeter

now she is raising herself
graceful as a ballerina
hands and arms outstretched
she pirouettes, a joyous twirl

releasing and dispersing yesterday's
muddied water, and in this act
I suddenly see who she might have been
before she lost herself

to feral cats and black crows, they know
and bear witness as she wipes the dish clean
adds fresh water and bends again
to feed the hungry

felines emerging from the bamboo stalks
and the birds too, heaving themselves
out of trees, herding their young
the way we all do

as shadows multiply the black wings
circling round her head
reminding me, who has no use
for feral cats and black crows
everything is sacrament.

-Marion Goldstein

Prayer

Prayer formed a thin grey line
above the elephants drowsing
      in the grass,
a coating almost, as the elephants drowsed,
standing on their own four legs,
      their ancient legs,
asking for nothing as the world
went on or by.

And a war was happening
      in the pit of the stomach
that is the world,
as fires raged and somewhere,
a flame burned in a window somewhere
      in Nantucket
or Halifax or Nova Scotia
or Athens, Georgia.

The elephants dreamed standing up,
breathing long, soft, wet breaths
      through their trunks,
each pink at the end and like
a mouth or a hand pulling up
      a flower or a weed
as they breathed, the thin line
of prayer above them.

And God, a great cornea, looking
down on the stomach that is earth
          into the pit that is war
as a doubtful peace tossed
in the air like a bird,
          or a bird broken
into smaller birds, the heavens waiting
for the wars, the wars waiting
          for the heavens.

While a grandmother rocks
back and forth and back and forth
          in a chair, at a window,
with a candle on the sill,
in Nantucket or Halifax or Nova Scotia
          or Athens, Georgia.
Her mouth dry from age and from
waiting, feeling the grey of hope
or prayer like some thin line
          or canopy.

The elephants of the world dreaming,
in the pits of their stomachs,
          of grass.

                                        -Jon Pearson

During our Spiritual Poetry Writing Workshops, we look at poems from different eras and different religious traditions and use special prompts to seed our own writing. This is a small sampling of some of the poems used since we began:

◻ Unison benediction by May Sarton

◻ Saviour by Maya Angelou

◻ Untitled by Mirabai (16th century Hindu poet)

◻ Making Peace by Denise Levertov

◻ Imagine by John Lennon

◻ A cushion for your head by Hafiz (14th century Persian poet, trans. by Daniel Landinsky)

◻ The dark by Wendell Berry

◻ We lived happily during the war by Ilya Kaminsky (Ukrainian-American Poet)

◻ Desert Tears by Stewart Bitkoff (Contemporary sufi poet)

◻ Jerusalem: Passover, Easter by Stanley Moss

◻ Tree by Jane Hirshfield

◻ The World Has Need of You by Ellen Bass

◻ What a human is now I know by Muhittin Abdal (13th c. Turkish Muslim poet trans. by Jennifer Ferraro & Latif Bolat)

◻ Just now by W.S. Merwin

◻ Between the fires by Rabbi Arthur Waskow

◻ You who let yourselves feel: enter the breathing by Rainer Maria Rilke

◻ FOR THE SLEEPWALKERS by Edward Hirsch

◻ The laughing heart by Charles Bukowski (poet, novelist, short story writer, L.A.)

- What to remember when waking by David Whyte
- Stone by Danusha Lameris
- Clearly by James Crews (contemporary poet from Missouri)
- I've learned to live simply, wisely by Anna Akhmatova
- Flute Song by Rumi
- I Thought I'd Awaken To by Amanda Gorman
- Saint Francis and the Sow by Galway Kinnel
- Love after Love by Derek Walcott
- Poetic by A.R. Ammons
- The Gate by Marie Howe
- IT WAS LIKE A STREAM by AKKA Mahadevi (12th century India)
- One heart by Li-Young Lee
- A single word can brighten the face by Yunus Emre (Turkish Muslim poet 13th-14th centuries)
- Try to Praise the Mutilated World by Adam Zagajewski
- Among the multitudes by Wislawa Szymborska
- I climb the road to cold mountain by Han Shan (9th century Taoist poet)
- This snowy morning by Matsuo Basho (17th century Japanese Buddhist poet, trans. by Peter Beilenson)
- Full Moon Festival by Thich Nhat Hanh
- I Want to Know by Christine Valters Painter
- "Hope" is the thing with feathers by Emily Dickinson
- The Poet's Obligation by Pablo Neruda
- From leaves of grass by Walt Whitman
- What they did yesterday afternoon by Warshan Shire (contemporary African Poet from Somali and London)
- Expands his being by Meister Eckhart (German Christian Mystic of 13th century)

- ¤ That Much Closer by Adele Kenny
- ¤ For calling the spirit back from wandering the earth in its human feet by Joy Harjo (U.S. Poet Laureate 2019-2022)
- ¤ Instructions on Not Giving Up by Ada Limon
- ¤ A fish cannot drown in water by Mechtild of Magdeburg (13th century Christian mystic)
- ¤ Mindful by Mary Oliver
- ¤ The Pathway Finally Opened by Mahsati Ganjavi (12th century Muslim poet)
- ¤ Now That We Have Tasted Hope by Khaled Mattawa (contemporary Libyan poet)
- ¤ Digging by Seamus Heaney
- ¤ Cutting loose by William Stafford

About the Spiritual Poetry Workshops

In the calm kindness that Donna creates, she takes us deep into spiritual poems from across the centuries. From these inspirations, she draws possible prompts. Each poet in the room is a gifted writer, which makes listening to their poems a remarkable artistic experience. That could have been intimidating, but the magic that happens here seems to arise from everyone's openheartedness. Each person brings such specific wisdom and grace, and such distinct voice, rhythm, and sensibility, that I am continually transported and charmed. We are fellow searchers following different paths.

It turns out, for me, that "spiritual poetry" isn't writing directly about the Divine, which shines blindingly bright and too monumental to fit into my limited, linear mind. When I've tried to narrate a moment of Holy Presence, tried to capture it in my lines, they become like the bars of a cage. Not only do I have no earthly (or heavenly) right to try to tame a magnificent Wildness, but also the Spirit I want only to love better disappears, reduced to previously known phenomena, neutered by craft.

If I look directly at the Sun, I'll lose my sight. If I squint too narrowly at God, I'll risk losing a wondrous Gift. Instead, here with Donna and travelers from different traditions, I'm learning to search for deep heartbeat and healing breath, for footprints and echoes, for seeds and remains, for the wind that blows Grace my way. It's not an overstatement to say this class has been a revelation..

-*Molly Howes*

CONTRIBUTORS

VINITA AGRAWAL

Vinita Agrawal is the author of four books of poetry. Her forthcoming collection *Twilight Language* is a finalist at the Proverse Prize, 2021, Hongkong. She has edited an anthology on climate change titled *Open Your Eyes* (Hawakal) and Co-edited two volumes of the *Yearbook of Indian Poetry in English* (Hawakal). She was jointly awarded the Tagore Literary Prize in 2018. She is on the Global Judging Panel of the SheInsprawrds. www.vinitawords.com

RICKI AIELLO

Ricki Aiello is a New England writer. Her publishing credits include personal essays in the magazine *Front Porch Review,* non-fiction devotional pieces in *The Upper Room and Christian Century,* a submission to the International Women Writers Guild magazine, *Network,* and a short story, *Remember When* accepted in a new launch, *Portrait of New England.* Currently, she is writing memoir essays focused on her relationship with her mother as well as another book of essays exploring those odd moments in life that teach us something unexpected. When not writing, she enjoys reading anything and everything. Memoirs have become a special favorite. She also enjoys a new love for poetry.

KAY ALLGOOD

Kay Allgood's interest in word-crafting and poetry began when she was introduced to e.e. cummings and Dorothy Parker in high school but writing in earnest began much later. She has taught workshops on writing poetry to youth and adults; collaborated with a book-maker's art project on the theme "Pupil of the Eye", referring to 'blackness' being where the light gets in; and also contributed poetry to a retiring photography professor's retrospective exhibit. She especially enjoys collaborations between various arts modalities. Formally publishing her own work is a work in progress!

CIT ANANDA

Cit Ananda Fowler, DDiv., experiences language as a proxy pointing to the mystical elegance of life. Her poetry is inspired by direct experience, captured in moments between perception when the mind falls quiet. She will tell you she catches poetry on the winds of the universe. She lives with her husband, two children, a fox-red lab, a rescue cat and a calico bunny in Idaho. Cit Ananda has work published or forthcoming in *Mountain Path, Tiferet Journal, Amethyst Review* and *Soul-Lit*. Explore more at https://ww.vitalrootsherbalism.com/publications.

ELYA BRADEN

Elya Braden is the author of the chapbooks *Open The Fist*, released in 2020, and *The Sight of Invisible Longing*, coming out in 2023, both by Finishing Line Press. She is a writer and mixed-media artist living in Ventura County, CA, and is Assistant Editor of *Gyroscope Review*. Her work has been widely published, and her poems have received a Pushcart Prize nomination and several Best of the Net nominations. www.elyabraden.com.

DAVID BREITKOPF

David Breitkopf has been a professional tennis player and coach, a journalist for many years, and a professional standup comic back in the 1990s. He currently teaches English in an upstate New York high school. Despite these jobs, David has managed to write poetry, fiction, some of which has been published in various literary magazines, and even a few plays. For the past three years, David has been toiling over a short epic poem, or rhapsody dealing with spiritual matters.

ROSE BROMBERG

Rose Bromberg is the author of two poetry chapbooks whose themes span the world of nature and the field of medicine: *The Language of Seasons* (Finishing Line Press, 2018) and *Poemedica* (Finishing Line Press, 2011), which was a finalist in FLP's Poetry Chapbook Competition. Rose is a Pushcart Prize nominee and her work has appeared in numerous journals and anthologies such as *RUNE* (The MIT Journal of Arts and Letters), *Medscape J Med., Bridges, Southern Indiana Review, Tipton Poetry Journal, rock & sling* and elsewhere.

SIMON CONSTAM

Simon Constam is a Toronto poet and aphorist. His first book of poetry, *Brought Down*, was published in January 2022, by Wipf and Stock Publishers. Its early reviews have been exceptional! He has published poetry in a number of magazines among them *The Jewish Literary Journal, long con magazine, the Dark Poets Club* and *Poetica Magazine*. Since late 2018, he has been publishing, under the moniker Daily Ferocity, a new, original aphorism every day on Instagram and for an email subscriber base. See more about Simon at simonconstam.com

MARGARET COOMBS

Margaret Coombs is a poet and retired academic librarian from Manitowoc, Wisconsin. Her first chapbook, *The Joy of Their Holiness*, was published in 2020 under the name Peggy Turnbull. She now uses her birth name as her pen name to honor the poet she was as a young woman. Some of her recent poems have appeared in *Amethyst Review, Verse-Virtual*, and *Bramble*. She is a member of the Wisconsin Fellowship of Poets, the International Women's Writing Guild, and the Science Fiction Poetry Association.

JONI ELENA DAIDONE

Joni Elena Daidone is a writer and creative activist living between New York City and the Harlem Valley. She writes ekphrastic prose poems, short fiction, one-act plays and monologues as a way to connect to the divine and as a voice for the silent feminine spirit. She's worked in educational publishing, media, and communications for 30+ years. Joni teaches ESL writing to immigrants through various community programs, including working with High School Seniors through the PEN America Writing program. She recently completed a book of Ekphrastic prose poetry celebrating the art of her late husband, Brian Saltern, and is completing a second book *My Women, My Tribe* based on the photos and stories of women ancestors and mentors whose indomitable spirits inspired her. Contact: joniwriter@gmail.com Instagram: @joandaidone

TERRY DAVIS

Terry Davis is returning to writing poetry after a long absence. A former communications consultant for Fortune 1000 companies who became an ordained Unitarian Universalist minister at age 50, Terry is rediscovering her own connection to mystery through poetry. Terry is a graduate of Candler School of Theology at Emory University in Atlanta. She received her certification in spiritual direction from the Haden Institute, which offers a Jungian-based intensive course of study. Based in Asheville, North Carolina, Terry serves as the minister of the Unitarian Universalist Fellowship of Hendersonville (starting September 1, 2022).

MARGO JODYNE DILLS
With a Certificate in Writing from University of Washington, Margo Jodyne Dills is an active member of Hugo House and Epic Write in Seattle. Her friends call her Jodi. She lives in Seattle with her chihuahua rescue, Penny Lane, and manages an 80-unit apartment building in her spare time. Like many, she writes because she must. Jodi does not write in one genre and admits she is kind of all over the place but learning so much in the process. *Nail Set* is the title poem of her first chapbook, which covers a period in her life of tragic changes and eye-opening discoveries.

SUZANNE DOERGE
Suzanne Doerge guides creative writing workshops with multicultural groups of women and youth, as a facilitator in the AWA (Amherst Writers and Artists) method. Her poems have been published in several journals and anthology, in print and on-line. *Footfalls: Poems of the Camino,* her first collection of poetry, released in 2022 by Shanti Arts Publishing, traces her reflections when walking the Camino de Santiago in Spain. She lives in Ottawa, Ontario, Canada, on the unceded land of the Algonquin people. www.ripplingwaters.ca

ALLISON DOUGLAS-TOURNER
Allison Douglas-Tourner lives on Vancouver Island. Her poetry has also been published in *Island Writers' Magazine, The Antigonish Review,* and *Pensive.* Her short form poems have appeared in *The Poetry Pea Journal, The Wales Haiku Journal, Tsuridoro,* and *Haiku Universe.*

TAMMY EINSTEIN
Dr Tamar Einstein, (Tammy), is a mother, an Expressive Arts Therapist, writer, jewelry designer, dancer and artist in Jerusalem.
Her love of writing began in early childhood in a Manhattan. Public school intriguingly named "The Emily Dickenson School". Her immersion in the arts is a daily part of her spiritual, professional, and academic life. Her doctoral research and lifelong passion: Multiculturalism and Expressive Arts Therapy in Jerusalem are at the heart of her work. The Tiferet Journal Online Spiritual Poetry class has become a home and it is

a blessing and honor to share this dwelling space with other welcoming and open-hearted poets. Once again, the arts provide a space for healing and holding.

ALICIA ELKORT

Alicia Elkort (she/her) has been nominated thrice for the Pushcart, twice for Best of the Net and once for the Orisons Anthology. Her first book of poetry, *A Map of Every Undoing*, was published in the fall of 2022 by Still-house Press with George Mason University, and she has been published in numerous journals and anthologies. She reads for *Tinderbox Poetry Journal* and works as a Life Coach and as an editor with Shiversong LLC. Alicia lives in the gorgeous light of Santa Fe, NM. For more info or to watch her two video poems: http://aliciaelkort.mystrikingly.com/

DORIS FERLEGER

Doris Ferleger, Ph.D., a former poet Laureate of Montgomery County PA, and award-winning poet and memoir essayist, is the author of four full length volumes entitled: *Big Silences in a Year of Rain, As the Moon Has Breath, Leavened*, and *As for the Kiss*, (finalist for Marsh Hawk Poetry Prize and Cod Hill Poetry Prize), and a chapbook entitled *When You Become Snow*. Ferleger's work has been published in numerous journals including *Cimarron Review, L.A. Review, South Carolina Review* and *Poet Lore*. Aliki Barnestone writes: These memorable poems keep singing with their insistent beauty.

LUCINDA GADOW

Lucinda Gadow is a NonDual Kabbalistic Healer. The nature of her studies for the past twenty-one years has been in the realm of spirituality. The Writing Circle has offered her the opportunity to explore a variety of writing experiences. Ms. Gadow lives on Long Island's north shore which is often an inspiration for her poetry.

DEBORAH GERRISH

Deborah Gerrish is the author of three collections of poems, *Light in Light* (2017), *The Language of Paisley* (2012), and the chapbook, *The Language of Rain* (2008). She was awarded an Edward Fry Fellowship and received an EDD from Rutger's University in Literacy Education. She holds an MFA in Poetry from Drew University, teaches poetry workshops at Fairleigh Dickinson University, and organizes readings for Visiting Poets. Her new poetry collection, *Indeed Jasmine*, will be forthcoming in 2022.

MARIA GIURA

Maria Giura is the author of *Celibate: A Memoir*, which won a 2020 First Place Independent Press Award, and *What My Father Taught Me*, which was a finalist for the Paterson Poetry Book Award. Her writing has appeared in several journals including *Prime Number, Presence, Vita Poetica, (Voices in) Italian Americana, Tiferet, Lips* and the *Paterson Literary Review*. An Academy of American Poets winner, Maria has taught writing at multiple universities including Binghamton University where she earned her PhD in English. She currently teaches memoir workshops for Casa Belvedere Cultural Foundation. Follow her on Instagram @marigiurawrites and at mariagiura.com

MARION GOLDSTEIN

Marion Goldstein is a psychotherapist and author of a poetry collection, *Architecture of the Unpronounced*, and two memoirs *Hard to Place* and *Embracing the Sign*, all published by North Star Press. Her two chapbooks are, *Psalms for The Cosmos*, which won the Red Wheelbarrow Award and *Blue Prints*. Her poetry and essays have been published in literary journals, newspapers, and anthologies, such as *Ars Medica, The Watershed Review, America, Friend's Journal, Adanna, Memory House, The Christian Science Monitor* and *Presence*.

PAMELA GOTTFRIED

Pamela Jay Gottfried is a rabbi and lifelong learner who lives in Metro Atlanta and serves as the Scholar-in-Residence at The Weber School, a Jewish Community High School. She is the author of *Found in Translation: Common Words of Uncommon Wisdom*, and is currently working on a collection of stories and poems about her 25+ years as a parent and teacher. In addition to attending Tiferet's Spiritual Poetry Writing classes, Pamela spends her free time throwing pots in the ceramics studio, reading novels, solving crosswords, playing Scrabble with her spouse, and taking walks with her canine companion, Henry.

ELIZABETH GRAHAM

Elizabeth Ahyin Graham holds a BA in Journalism from the University of Texas at Austin and an MA in Transformative Leadership from California Institute of Integral Studies. In 2019, Elizabeth stepped away from her Integrative Neuromuscular Therapy practice of 30 years in the SF Bay Area and is transitioning her work into a career in technical writing.

Concurrently, she is working on an educational project to teach deepening being and presence based on her life's work in clinical therapy. Writing is a daily part of her contemplative life, creative and generative process of awareness.

MELANIE LYNN GRIFFIN

Melanie Lynn Griffin holds a Masters in Creative Nonfiction from Johns Hopkins University and a Certificate in Spiritual Direction from National Cathedral College. After several decades lobbying for Sierra Club on Capitol Hill, she now enjoys leading retreats and workshops in the D.C. area. Her publishing credits include *Sierra magazine, Sojourners, AARP Bulletin*, and *So to Speak Journal*. For links to publications and her blog, Writing with Spirit, visit https://melanielynngriffin.contently.com/

MARIJO GROGAN

Marijo Grogan is a psychotherapist and teacher whose writing has been published in *Sojourner Magazine, The American Humanistic Psychology Review, Braided Way, In Drought Times*, and *Landslide*. Her award-winning play was performed at the Heartlande Festival and an essay was broadcast on National Public Radio. She contributed a chapter to *EmbodyKind* published by BraveHealer in September 2022. Her creative non-fiction will appear in a future publication of *HerStry*.

J.M.R. HARRISON

J.M.R. Harrison has created and led workshops in fear, faith, poetry, play, and creativity. She studied poetry at the independent Writers' Center in Bethesda MD for over a dozen years and is a 2016 graduate from the low residency MFA program of Spalding University in Louisville KY. Her poems have been published in *Antietam Review, Spillway Magazine, Pensive Journal* and featured in *Fluent Magazine* and *The Good Newspaper*.

THOMAS HEDT

Thomas Hedt lives in Eureka, California. His poetry has appeared in: *The Sijo International Journal of Poetry and Song, The Tule Review, The Lilly Poetry Review, Cathexis NW*, and elsewhere. His first compilation, *Artifacts and Assorted Memorabilia*, was released in September of 2020 by Cold River Press.

DUANE L HERRMANN

Internationally published, award-winning poet and historian, Duane L Herrmann has work translated into several languages, published in a dozen countries, in print and online. He has eight full-length collections of poetry, a sci fi novel, a history book, and more chapbooks. His poetry has received the Robert Hayden Poetry Fellowship, inclusion in *American Poets of the 1990s*, Map of Kansas Literature (website), Kansas Poets Trail and others. These accomplishments defy Duane's traumatic childhood embellished by dyslexia, ADHD and, now, PTSD. He spends his time on the prairie with trees in the breeze and writes – and loves moonlight!

CHRISTINE HIGGINS

Christine Higgins is the author of *Hallow*, a full-length collection of poetry published in Spring, 2020 (Cherry Grove). She was the 2nd place winner in the Poetry Box competition for her chapbook, *Hello, Darling* in 2019. She is the co-author of *In the Margins, A Conversation in Poetry* (Cherry Grove, 2017). She has been the recipient of a Maryland State Arts Council Award for both poetry and non-fiction. Her work has appeared in *America, Poetry East, Nagautuck River Review* and *Windhover*. You can read more about her on her website: www.christinehigginswriter.com.

JANET HILLER

Dr. Janet Hiller was born after WWII in Bergen Belsen, then a displaced persons camp. Her parents were both Holocaust survivors. Janet earned a doctorate in Linguistics and Modern Language Pedagogy from Stony Brook University. She raised three amazing children, became a school administrator and an associate professor at Long Island University. Janet is a textbook author and wrote numerous articles for professional journals. Her poetry has been published in *The Jewish Literary Journal*. Janet volunteers at the Jewish Federation of Sarasota-Manatee. Part of their Speaker's Bureau, she educates the community about the Holocaust as her mother did before her.

MOLLY HOWES

Molly Howes's nonfiction has appeared in *The New York Times* "Modern Love" column, *Boston Globe Magazine, Bellingham Review, Tampa Review*, and other publications; and was listed as Notable in Best American Essays. Her 2020 nonfiction book *A Good Apology* explores the meaning and power of making amends. She's the grateful recipient of fellowships at Ragdale, VCCA, A Room of Her Own, and MacDowell. Although she's lived in New England for decades, she returns to the Gulf of Mexico every chance she gets. Her work as a clinical psychologist and her life with children have taught her how to think and love.

GABRIELA IÑIGUEZ

Gabriela Iñiguez is a poet and a graduate student at San Jose State University. She has more than ten years of experience as a high school math teacher. Her most recent publication is her book *Moments of Inspiration Momentos de Inspiración Poetry* written in English and Spanish which she personally translated in both languages. Her poetry is inspired by life's magical moments, and she hopes to inspire you with her words. For more information contact her at: gabrielainiguez.poet@gmail.com.

SUSAN JACKSON

Susan Jackson's new poetry collection *In the River of Songs* was published in May 2022 by CavanKerry Press. She is the author of *Through a Gate of Trees* (also CKP) and the chapbook *All the Light in Between* (Finishing Line Press). Jackson received a Fellowship Grant from the New Jersey State Council on the Arts, as well as residency grants to to Vermont Studio Center and Virginia Center for the Creative Arts. She co-leads the summer program "Poetry as Spiritual Practice" in Teton County, Wyoming. This summer's theme was "Seeing Through the Eye of the Heart." Jackson is grateful to be part of the Tiferet community of writers.

TERESA H. JANSSEN

Teresa H. Janssen's prose has been designated a notable in The Best American Essays and has received the Norman Mailer/NCTE creative nonfiction award for high school teachers. Her writing has appeared in *Zyzzyva, Tiferet, Parabola, Ruminate, Los Angeles Review, Anchor Magazine, Under the Sun*, and elsewhere. She lives in Washington State where she tends a small orchard and writes about nature, spirituality, and social issues. She can be found online at www.teresahjanssen.com.

NANCY K. JENTSCH

Nancy K. Jentsch's poetry has appeared recently in *The Pine Cone Review, Scissortail Quarterly, Third Wednesday* and *Tipton Poetry Journal* and in the anthologies *Riparian* (Dos Madres Press) and *A Walk with Nature* (University Professors Press). Poems written in the workshops have been published or are forthcoming in *Amethyst Review, Verse-Virtual* and *Zingara Poetry Review*, In 2020, she received an Arts Enrichment Grant from the

Kentucky Foundation for Women. Her chapbook, *Authorized Visitors*, was published in 2017 (Cherry Grove Collections) and *Between the Rows*, her first poetry collection, is available from Shanti Arts. More information is available at her website, https://jentsch8.wixsite.com/my-site.

BETTY JOHNSON

Betty Johnson lives in Shreveport, LA; since retiring from a career in healthcare she divides her time between gardening, sharing coffee with friends, camping, and occasionally writing a poem. She facilitates writing circles where self exploration and growth can be done in a safe space. Spiritual practices include yoga, journaling, knitting and tending the earth.

GAIL H KAPLAN

Gail H Kaplan attended the University of Texas in Austin. After graduating in 1973, she joined the Peace Corps and spent three years in Africa. During that time, Gail asked her students to tell her stories about their childhood and she wrote a book about their tales. When she returned to the US, Gail was a teacher for 3 years and then became a Recruiter for Patent Attorneys. During COVID, she took many poetry and prose classes and found that she has a passion for writing.

BAMBI KOENIGER

Rev. Bambi Smithers Koeniger is a retired Episcopal priest and a non dual healer who loves to write, read, sing, hike and dance. During this pandemic, time slowed down and stillness became a daily practice. The offer of this Spiritual Poetry class has been such a gift. Donna Baer Stein as the instructor offers such amazing space to reveal our souls desire. All the students have enriched my life as well. We look forward to our time together each week as we write and hear each others open hearts beam into pearls of wisdom.

MAGIN LASOV GREGG

Magin LaSov Gregg's essays have appeared in *The Washington Post, National Public Radio, The Rumpus, Bellingham Review, Hippocampus Magazine, Full Grown People, Solstice Literary Magazine, Under the Gum Tree,* and elsewhere. Her essay *This Altar in My Heart* was a creative nonfiction finalist in Tiferet Journal's 2021 Contest. Other work has been nominated for a Pushcart Prize and featured at Memoir Monday. Magin began writ-

163

ing poetry in 2021 and has published a few pieces at *Anti-Heroin Chic* and *Sledgehammer Literary Journal*. She lives with her husband, Carl, and four fabulous pets in a slightly haunted house in Frederick, Maryland.

SARA LETOURNEAU

Sara Letourneau is a poet as well as a book editor, literary coach, and writing workshop instructor. Her poetry has appeared or is forthcoming in *Living Crue, ArLiJo (Arlington Literary Journal), Mass Poetry's Poem of the Moment and Hard Work of Hope, Muddy River Poetry Review, Boston Small Press and Poetry Scene, Soul-Lit, Amethyst Review, Constellations*, and *The Aurorean*, among others. Her manuscript for her first full-length poetry collection is on submission. She lives in southeastern Massachusetts, though she also frequents southern New Hampshire and Cape Cod. Learn more about Sara and her work at https://heartofthestoryeditorial. com.

ALEXANDER LEVERING KERN

Alexander Levering Kern is a poet, writer, editor, Quaker educator, and interfaith chaplain who serves as Executive Director of the Center for Spirituality, Dialogue, and Service at Northeastern University in Boston. Editor of the anthology, *Becoming Fire: Spiritual Writing from Rising Generations*, his work appears in publications such as *CONSEQUENCE Online, Georgetown Review, About Place Journal, Journal of* the American Medical Association (JAMA), and anthologies from Main Street Rag, Ibbetson Street, Pudding House and more. Founding co-editor of Pensive: A Global Journal of Spirituality and the Arts (www.pensivejournal.com), he lives in Somerville, Massachusetts with his spouse Rebecca and children Elias and Ruthanna.

LYNDA LEVY

Lynda Levy is a retired psychologist and life coach. After living in Los Angeles for most of her adult life, she's relocated to Phoenix, Arizona, where she's found that much blooms in the desert, including her own creativity. Her work has appeared in *The Sonder Review, 9 Lives: A Life in 10 Minutes Anthology*, and *Feminine Rising: Voices of Power and Invisibility*.

SUSAN L. LIPSON

Susan L. Lipson is a poet, singer-songwriter, self-employed creative writing teacher, and author of fiction and educational materials for children. Her poems have appeared individually in *Rattle Magazine, Haunted Waters Press, Scapegoat Review, Plants & Poetry Journal, The San Diego Union-Tri-*

bune, and the *Jewish Writing Project* blog, and as collections in a poetry book called *Disillusions of Grandeur and Other Eye- Openers* (Amazon), and within a textbook, *Writing Success Through Poetry* (Prufrock Press). Her forthcoming music album, "Songs for Divine Conversations," will feature 12 original songs, many of which she sings regularly as a cantorial soloist. Read more at https://susanllipsonwordsandmusic.com.

JANICE LORE

Janice Lore's writing has appeared in various anthologies and literary magazines, and on CBC radio. Her poetry chapbook, *Ipsissima Verba,* (a "found" poem about math, philosophy, definitions and a middle-aged woman's life), was also scripted and performed. She wrote her first commissioned work, *Requiem for the Fridge,* on the door of a dead refrigerator. Janice is inspired by working with other artists and has collaborated on several multi-disciplinary performances. She also makes handmade books.

KAREN LUKE JACKSON

Karen Luke Jackson draws upon oral history, contemplative practices, and nature for inspiration. Her poems have appeared in numerous journals including *Broad River Review* (Rash Poetry Award), *Ruminate, One,* and *Friends Journal.* Her chapbook *GRIT* (Finishing Line Press, 2020) chronicles her sister's ventures as an award-winning clown and her full collection *The View Ever Changing* (Kelsay Books, 2021) explores the power of place and family ties. A lover of trees, Karen resides in a cottage on a goat pasture in Flat Rock, NC. When she's not writing, she companions people on their spiritual journeys. www.karenlukejackson.com

HELEN MAZARAKIS

Helen Mazarakis has been writing all her life, but especially in the past decade. She gains great support from a workshopping group, the Lady Mechanics, and from Donna's Spiritual Poetry Writing Classes, which has been a source of inspiration and awe. Her poems have been published in *Moonstone, Exit 13, Clementine,* and *Everyday Poets,* among others. A former community development specialist, Helen still serves on several non-profit boards that support and build community and opportunity. She has three grown children, and lives in her empty nest in Montclair NJ with her husband and two faithful dogs.

MARILYN MOHR

Marilyn Mohr is the author of two volumes of poetry, *Satchel* (Cross Cultural Communications Press, Merrick, NY, 1992), and *Running the Track* (Aesopus Press, Woodstock, NY 1981). She has been published in numerous magazines and anthologies, and has performed her work on radio and television. Her recent work can be seen in the *Paterson Literary Review, Poets on the Verge, The Paterson Literary Review* and *Lips Magazine*. A native New Yorker, she lived in Woodstock, where she was co-editor of *The Woodstock Poetry Review* and *The Catskill Poets' Series*. She was the coordinator of The Poets' Forum at the JCC of Metropolitan New Jersey. She lives in West Orange, New Jersey.

MARY-LYNNE MONROE

Mary-Lynne Monroe wrote poetry, memoir, flash fiction and nonfiction. She was published in *Offerings: Poems Written During Tiferet Journal's Spiritual Poetry Class, Vol. 2* and *Vol. 3; 2020 Writing from Inlandia; The Power of Our Voices: Sharing Our Story*; and *Opening the Gate*, an anthology. Her blog Unfolding Myths, which she contributed to for many years can be found at https://unfoldingmyths.blogspot.com.

LEAH C MUELLER

Leah C Mueller is an educator and consultant who worked 30+ years in Alberta, Canada. She completed her Masters of Arts in At Risk Youth and worked with at risk students, ranging from K-12, and their families. Her experiences include classroom teacher, resource teacher, learning/curriculum leader, special education consultant and behavior consultant. Leah is also a photographer and has taught photography classes to children and teens. She is devoted to family, photography, writing, painting and creating. Being retired and having valuable time to dedicate to all of these have left her giddy with possibilities.

MARLA MULLOY

Marla Mulloy is a writer with an evolving collection of essays, poems and stories, having been recently published in *The Timberline Review, Brevity Blog* and *Ruminate Magazine.* She has been a teacher and now works with refugees in Calgary, Alberta, Canada. Her writing reflects the experience of those who are finding refuge in new places, including relationship; seeking harmony in life as it is. Some of her writing is shared through her blog: www.tossingwords.wordpress.com.

LOUISA MUNIZ

Louisa Muniz lives in Sayreville, N.J. She holds a Master's in Curriculum and Instruction from Kean University. Her work has appeared in *Tinderbox Journal, Palette Poetry, SWWIM, Poetry Quarterly, PANK Magazine, Jabberwock Review* and elsewhere. She won the Sheila-Na-Gig 2019 Spring Contest for her poem *Stone Turned Sand*. Her work has been nominated for Best of the Net and a Pushcart Prize. Her debut chapbook, After Heavy Rains by Finishing Line Press was released in December, 2020.

NITYA NEDYAM

Nitya Nedyam is a Southeast Asian poet and woman of colour currently living in Singapore. Her poem *Self-Portrait* was a winner at the Poetry Festival Singapore's Catharsis 2021 competition. Her poems have also appeared in the literary anthology *Offshoots 15* (2020) and the *Tiferet Journal Chapbook Offerings III* (2021). She has a published recipe in *Flavours of Friendship: A Blend of Recipes* from SATS and *Around the World* (2019). She has a poem forthcoming in the publication *What We Inherit: Growing Up Indian* (2022).

SHARON NEUBAUER

Sharon Neubauer is a poet, playwright, yoga instructor and studio owner living in the Washington DC area. She has an English degree from Dickinson College. Sharon's first chapbook *Work of Body: Body of Work* is expected out in 2023, published by Finishing Line Press. She believes that creative ideas float in the air and that we need to open ourselves to catch them. She is deeply grateful to *Tiferet Journal* for their inspiration, classes, and encouragement.

JANE O'SHIELDS

Jane O'Shields is a writer and visual artist who lives in the foothills of the Santa Ana Mountains in Southern California. Jane writes non-fiction, fiction and poetry and she is currently completing a triptych of short stories called *An Unwavering Band of Light* en homage to Kurt Vonnegut, Jr. She describes her writing and visual art as aspects of the same need and Jane is adept in creating images that tell their stories and stories that paint their images. Jane holds a Bachelor's degree from Texas Christian University in art and Education, and a Master's degree in Occupational Therapy from Loma Linda University. She is an activist for peace and social justice and for three decades she has provided home health Occupational Therapy to home bound patients. Jane lives on the edge of a canyon she named

Blackwing. The wild nature of the animals and flora there, the water that runs from the ground and her view of the emotionally labile sky with its transient beauties inspires her and grounds her to what she is driven to create.

LYNN PALUMBO

Lynn Palumbo is a former graduate student in English (NYU), lover of Romantic poetry, Buddhist and devotee of arts and letters. Many of her poems come out of her practice of silence and observations of nature. She has been published by *The Avocet, A Journal of Nature Poetry* (USA) and *Urthona, A Journal of Buddhism and the Arts* (UK).

JON PEARSON

Jon Pearson is a writer, speaker, and artist. He was once a cartoonist for the *Oakland Tribune*, an extra for the New York Metropolitan Opera, a college professor, a mailman, and a piano mover. He has been published in numerous journals and nominated twice for the Pushcart Prize. He writes now for the same reason he played with his food as a kid — to make the world a better place. www.jonpearsoncreative.com

BILL RATNER

Bill Ratner's poetry is published in *Best Small Fictions 2021* (Sonder Press), chapbook: *To Decorate a Casket* (Finishing Line Press), full collection: *Fear of Fish* (Alien Buddha Press), *Rattle Magazine's Rattlecast, Missouri Review Audio, Baltimore Review, Chiron Review, Star*Line*, and other journals. Bill is a 9-time winner of The Moth StorySLAM, 2-time winner of Best of The Hollywood Fringe Extension Award for Solo Performance, a certified volunteer grief counsellor, and earns his living as a voice actor. https:// billratner.com/author • twitter.com/billratner • instagram.com/ billratner

SHELLEY RIO-GLICK

Shelley Rio-Glick is now retired. When working as a photographer, writer, social activist, clinician, and healer, she exhibited and published her writing and photographs in various venues, including *The Connection, Gallery 388, The Blatant Image, The Lesbian and Gay Parenting Guide, Families in Transition* and *Tiferet*. At age 51, she and her partner, River, expanded their family to raise two amazing kids. These days, she enjoys playing the ukulele, writing poetry, and doing what she can to help save our world. She lives with her partner in Albany, NY.

168

LYNDA RUSH MYERS

Lynda Myer's roots are in education, as a high school English teacher and, later, as a teacher of English as a Second Language for Catholic Charities. Lynda is a life-long learner, educator, poet, and mixed media artist. Her work has been published by *The Poet* (Faith, Vol. 1, Spring 2021), *Craven Arts Council & Gallery* (New Bern, NC), *Christians in the Visual Arts* (CIVA), *EDGE of Faith* magazine and *Tiferet Journal* (2020, 2021), among others. She was awarded first prize in The UVA Medical Center's literary magazine for her mixed-media artwork in 2017. Lynda is the author of one poetry chapbook, *Low Country Roots, Book One*. She is diligently working on a poetry manuscript for 2023.

PERVIN SAKET

Pervin Saket was awarded the Srinivas Rayaprol Poetry Prize 2021 and was the inaugural Fellow for the Vancouver Manuscript Intensive 2021. Her novel *Urmila* has been adapted for the stage, featuring classical Indian dance forms. Her poems, including the collection *A Tinge of Turmeric*, have been featured in *Indian Quarterly, The Joao-Roque Literary Journal, Paris Lit Up, The Madras Courier, Borderless Journal, The Punch Magazine, Cold Noon, Tiferet Journal* and elsewhere. Pervin is the Poetry Editor of *The Bombay Literary Magazine* and cofounder of the annual Dum Pukht Writers' Workshop, Pondicherry, India.

ELLEN SAZZMAN

Ellen Sazzman is a Pushcart-nominated poet whose work has been published in many journals including *Another Chicago Magazine, the Mizmor Anthology, Poetry South, PANK, Connecticut River Review, Ekphrastic Review, WSQ, Sow's Ear, Lilith, Beltway Quarterly, Moment, Common Ground,* and *CALYX,* among others. Her collection *The Shomer* (Finishing Line Press) was a finalist for the Blue Lynx Prize and a semifinalist for the Elixir Press Antivenom Award and the Codhill Press Award. She received an honorable mention in the 2019 Ginsberg poetry contest, was shortlisted for the 2018 O'Donoghue Prize, and was awarded first place in Poetica's 2016 Rosenberg competition.

COLLETTE SELL

For most of her life, Collette Sell wrote only on things that could easily be lost - scraps of paper left in abandoned apartments or in the pockets of raggedy coats donated to Goodwill. She is blessed by the generosity of the fine poets of the Wednesday Tiferet Spiritual Writing Workshop; by founder and editor of *Tiferet Journal*, Donna Baier Stein; by coach, Judyth Hill; by Abby Wasserman at the O'Hanlon Center; and by teachers at The Grotto, San Francisco's esteemed gathering place for writers. With their help, she says, "I finally began to think that I could do this thing."

JOANELL SERRA
Joanell Serra is a poet, playwright, novelist and essayist from Northern California. Books include *The Vines We Planted* (Wido, 2018) and *(Her)oics Anthology*, a collection of women's essays about the pandemic (Regal House Publishing, 2021). Her work has won multiple writing contests. She is a student in the Randolph College MFA program.

AMY SMALL-MCKINNEY
Amy Small-McKinney is the author of two full-length books and three chapbooks. Her newest chapbook, *One Day I Am A Field*, was published by Glass Lyre Press (April, 2022). Her second full-length book of poems, *Walking Toward Cranes*, won the Kithara Book Prize (Glass Lyre Press, 2016). Small-McKinney's poems also appear in several anthologies, for example, *101 Jewish Poems for the Third Millennium*, Edited by Matthew E. Silverman and Nancy Naomi Carlson (Ashland Poetry Press). 2019, her poem *Birthplace* received Special Merits recognition by *The Comstock Review* for their Muriel Craft Bailey Poetry Contest, judged by poet, David Kirby, and again, 2021 for her poem, *Bench, Ducks, & Inn*, judged by poet, Juan Felipe Herrera. Her poems have also been translated into Korean and Romanian.

RAQUEL SOLOMON
Raquel Solomon is a poet, composer and songwriter. She studied flamenco guitar in Granada and also plays violin. She incorporates themes of family, music and Judaism in much of her writing. She has poetry published in *Mudfish, Spilt Ink, The Columbia Journal of American Studies, Voices Israel, The Bronx Memoir Project, Tiferet* chapbooks, and other literary journals. Most recently her poem, *Alef Beys* was chosen for the The David Labkovski Project, an online exhibit of paintings about Vilna, Lithuania. She is currently recording a song she composed to her grandfather's Yiddish poem with opera singer Cheryl Warfield, artistic director of More Opera in NYC. Her mother composed and will record the piano arrangement.

BETH WALKER

Beth Walker is a professional writing consultant at the University of Tennessee at Martin. Several of the drafts she began during *Tiferet's* poetry workshops have been published in *MomEgg Review* and *The Buddhist Poetry Review*. She also has been a finalist recently in the Hemingway Foundation's flash fiction contest and Minerva Rising's non-fiction chapbook competition, as well as *Tiferet's* annual writing competitions. Her essays appear in *Practical Composition* and *American Creative Non- Fiction*, among other book-length collections.

PAMELA WAX

Pamela Wax is the author of *Walking the Labyrinth* (Main Street Rag, 2022) and the forthcoming chapbook, *Starter Mothers* (Finishing Line Press). Her poems have received awards from *Crosswinds Poetry Journal, Paterson Literary Review, Oberon Poetry Magazine* and the Robinson Jeffers Tor House and have been published in many other journals. Her writings on Jewish spirituality, women's issues, and Mussar have also been widely published. Pam is a rabbi who facilitates workshops including spiritual poetry writing, Mussar, and Wise Aging. She walks labyrinths in the Northern Berkshires of Massachusetts and can be found at www.pamelawax.com.

SUSAN WHELEHAN

Susan Whelehan is a reader, writer, seeker, sister, Aries, artist, mother, wife and member of the League of Canadian Poets. Her favourite (okay, only, as of yet) poetry collection, *The Sky Laughs at Borders*, was published by Piquant Press in 2019. Woo-HOO! Other poems are in several anthologies, journals and friends' birthday cards. Susie was a runner-up in CBC's Canada Writes. She facilitates Amherst Writers and Artists workshops wherever she is invited and on-line. She can be reached at www.susiewhelehan.ca

THELMA WURZELBACHER

Thelma Wurzelbacher is a retired professor volunteering in her local community after many years in the capitol city of her state. Her career includes years in an architectural firm, decades teaching community college students, English Second Language adults, and corporate employees. Her lifetime goal is to live a service-based lifestyle within the mission of her religious congregation. She wants to see deeply the beauty of many subjects at the end of any lens. Her photos and poems are published "here and there."

LAURA ZACHARIN

Laura Zacharin is the author of *Common Brown House Moths* (Frontenac House 2019), longlisted for the 2020 Gerald Lampert Award. She has been the recipient of University of Toronto's Marina Nemat Award for Poetry, and Freefall's Micheline Maylor Prize. Her poetry has appeared in *The Fiddlehead, CV2, The Malahat Review, Prism, Arc Poetry,* and other Canadian literary journals. She lives in Toronto, Canada.

Made in the USA
Middletown, DE
20 January 2023

22344030R00096